A PHOTOGRAPHIC GUIDE TO

MAMMALS

OF SOUTHERN, CENTRAL
AND EAST AFRICA

CHRIS & MATHILDE STUART

Published by Struik Nature
(an imprint of Penguin Random House South Africa (Pty) Ltd)
Reg. No. 1953/000441/07
The Estuaries No. 4, Oxbow Crescent,
Century Avenue, Century City, 7441
PO Box 1144, Cape Town, 8000 South Africa

Visit **www.randomstruik.co.za** and join the Struik Nature Club
for updates, news, events and special offers

First published 1992
Second edition 2001
Third edition 2014

3 5 7 9 10 8 6 4 2

Front cover: Cheetah (Images of Africa/Andrew Bannister)
Back cover: Defassa Waterbuck (Chris & Mathilde Stuart)

Publisher: Pippa Parker
Project manager: Colette Alves
Designer: Neil Bester
Proofreader: Glynne Newlands

Reproduction by Hirt & Carter Cape (Pty) Ltd
Printing and binding: RR Donnelley Asia Printing Solutions Ltd

ISBN 978 1 77584 136 4 (PRINT)
ISBN 978 1 77584 146 3 (ePUB)
ISBN 978 1 77584 145 6 (ePDF)

CONTENTS

INTRODUCTION

One of the main attractions of southern, Central and East Africa is the great variety of game species and the impressively large herds that throng the open plains in many of its protected areas. Who could fail to be awed by the masses of migrating Blue Wildebeest at Serengeti, the concentrations of Hippopotamus in the Luangwa River, and the dry season gatherings of Elephant along the Chobe River. Usually it is the game and large predators that act as the prime attractions to the visitor but one cannot discount the extremely rich small animal fauna of the region. More than 1 000 species of mammal occur in Africa south of the Sahara Desert, most of these found in the area covered by this book.

Unlike bird-watching, mammal-watching presents a number of difficulties to the interested observer. Many of the smaller species – the bats, shrews, golden moles and small rodents – are nocturnal, secretive and seldom seen. However, you may on occasion observe bats at their roosts; shrews and mice are frequently caught by domestic cats and left as uneaten 'gifts'; and many of the species leave signs of their having passed: the meanderings of golden mole surface tunnels, mounds pushed up by molerats, small heaps of cut grass and sedge stems left by members of the *Otomys* species, and the tracks of the Water Mongoose in stream-side mud. All tell of the presence of these species in an area, and patience and perseverance may be rewarded with a sighting.

In this book we have covered 152 species of mammal: nearly all of the larger and more obvious species, also a few of the more unusual such as the Pangolin, Aardvark and Porcupine, as well as representatives from the different families and genera of bat, shrew, elephant shrew (sengi), golden mole and smaller rodents. In a guide of this nature there is not space enough to describe each of the small mammals but the notes will enable you to differentiate a horseshoe bat from a free-tailed bat and a shrew from an elephant shrew, for example. In many cases different species of bat, shrew, golden mole and some small rodents require careful examination of teeth and chromosomes to separate one from the other, and in such cases you will not be able to determine a specific mammal. There are areas of confusion and uncertainty even for the specialist: in the case of the Cape Serotine Bat some experts believe that several species may be involved and not just one. Even in the case of several larger species it is possible that further research will reveal more species are involved. This is the case with the Gorilla, with two species and four subspecies now recognized.

If one considers that a large number of the smaller species of mammal occurring in Africa are known from only a few specimens, one begins to realize how much research is still required. The Okapi was made known to the outside world only in 1900 and the Gorilla, although known for many centuries, was properly described only in the middle of the 19th century. Smaller species are still being discovered, such as the Longtailed Forest Shrew collected in 1978 in a forest on the southern coastal belt of South Africa. Several new species of rodent, mongoose and forest monkey have been described over the past 20 years.

A number of mammal species found in our area are threatened by hunting and habitat destruction. The Mountain Gorilla is restricted to small forest pockets and fewer than 750 survive today; fewer than 4 200 Eastern Lowland Gorilla roam the equatorial forest. The Black Rhinoceros numbers fewer than 4 300 individuals, and its future outside of southern Africa is bleak. One of Africa's most endangered mammals, the Riverine Rabbit, has seen much of its arid riverine scrub habitat destroyed by uncontrolled agriculture. The large carnivores have all decreased in number and this is particularly critical in the case of the Cheetah and the Wild Dog. Possibly fewer than 5 500 Wild Dog remain in the wild today and the Cheetah numbers fewer than 12 000, which is critically low for a species in the wild. Many other species – the Common Chimpanzee, Bonobo, Western Lowland Gorilla, Brown Hyaena, Lion, Grevy's Zebra, Hunter's Hartebeest and the Oribi – can be considered vulnerable. Elephant still occur in considerable numbers (probably fewer than 500 000) but the pressures of poaching and habitat destruction have resulted in dramatic declines in many areas over the past 20 years. Many species that appear to be abundant today may be gone tomorrow unless we take sensible action now. We need only remind ourselves that the Passenger Pigeon of North America, the Quagga of the South African plains, and the Dodo of Mauritius were once abundant but are now no more.

HOW TO USE THIS BOOK

This guide has been compiled with a view to the easy identification of the larger and more conspicuous mammals in southern, eastern and central Africa, as well as some of the smaller species. *Italic type* has been used to emphasize the key identification pointers where applicable. Photographs show differences between sexes where necessary, and portray young where they differ significantly from the adults; distinctly marked subspecies are also included.

Three different measurements have been used: total length (nose-tip to tail-tip) for smaller species, shoulder height for larger mammals, and wingspan for the bats. In addition to a brief description of each species, information on habitat is given to further aid identification. The distribution maps should be used to establish whether or not a particular species is present in a given area, and the thumbnail sketch key at the beginning of the book should help you determine to which group of mammals a species belongs, which will then guide you to the relevant pages. A habitat map of Africa shows the principal vegetation types on the continent.

ABBREVIATIONS

TL   Total Length
(nose-tip to tail-tip)

WS   Wingspan

SH   Shoulder Height

♀   Female

♂   Male

c.   circa

HABITATS

The vegetation map provided is, for practical purposes, a much simplified version of the real situation. Each individual area is in fact composed of many different vegetation types but such detail is unnecessarily complex for a book of this scope. Many species of mammal are restricted to one particular vegetation type or habitat, while some range over several types.

1. *Cape and Mediterranean evergreen scrub:* Found only in the extreme north-western and south-western corners of the continent, it is dominated by evergreen shrubs and bushes and is sometimes referred to as heathland, fynbos or macchia.

2. *Tropical rain forest:* The trees are predominantly evergreen and usually form a distinct canopy with a number of discrete vegetation strata. In West Africa particularly, large tracts have been destroyed.

3. *Desert:* The Sahara, by far the largest, dominates the north of the continent, and the Namib stretches down the south-western coast. These areas are characterized by very sparse vegetation and extremely low rainfall.

4. *Southern semi-desert:* This area includes the entire Kalahari, the Karoo, Bushmanland and Namaqualand. Vegetation ranges from open thorn-tree woodland to areas covered by short, woody shrubs and succulents.

5. *Montane areas:* These include the Atlas Mountains, the Ethiopian Highlands, the Ruwenzori range, Mt Kenya and

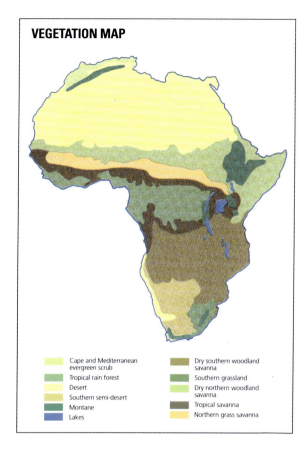

VEGETATION MAP

Cape and Mediterranean evergreen scrub	Dry southern woodland savanna
Tropical rain forest	Southern grassland
Desert	Dry northern woodland savanna
Southern semi-desert	Tropical savanna
Montane	Northern grass savanna
Lakes	

Mt Kilimanjaro, and the Drakensberg in the south. Vegetation varies considerably from range to range and includes forest, bamboo forest, grassland and various types of woodland.

6. *Dry southern and northern woodland savanna:* The northern areas tend to be drier than the southern but both contain elements of woodland, grassland and scrub. Trees are more abundant in the south and the grass is usually taller and denser.

7. *Southern grassland and northern grass savanna:* Grass species dominate with scatterings of trees, including acacias.

8 *Tropical savanna:* These comprise mixed grass and tree savanna and typically receive a fairly high rainfall. Some dense forest stands are scattered through these areas.

SUCCESSFUL MAMMAL-WATCHING

In order to observe the medium- to large-sized mammals you will require only a pair of binoculars, but if you wish to have a closer look at the smaller mammal species it is a good idea to obtain – or make – small live-traps. Trapping can be very time-consuming, however, and often a permit from the relevant conservation body will be required.

There are a number of basic steps to follow in order to identify a mammal once you have spotted it:

First try and establish to which group the animal belongs (is it an antelope, a dog or a cat, etc.?). Then make an estimate of shoulder height or, in the case of smaller species, total length and tail length (is the tail longer than the head and body length?). Are any features very obvious and thus distinguishing (a bushy or sparsely haired tail; spots or stripes; particularly long or short ears)? Make a note of general colour and any distinct markings.

In the case of an antelope be sure to note the shape of the horns and whether they are ridged, partly ridged or smooth. Bear in mind that young animals may in some cases resemble the adults of another species – particularly in early horn development. Make a note of any particular behavioural traits or peculiarities (was the animal in a large group or solitary? Was it in a tree? Did it enter a burrow?). Once you have sufficient information you can then consult the guide in order to try and establish what the particular species is.

A useful indicator of an animal's presence in an area is spoor or tracks, most easily seen in sand or mud, and also droppings. Fresh tracks may give you a clue as to what the animal was doing and may even lead to a glimpse of a more secretive species.

The distribution maps provided will also guide you by indicating whether or not a species occurs in a particular region. It is not probable, for example, that you would encounter a Gorilla in Zambia.

Habitat is a useful aid to identification too: you are not likely to see a Klipspringer on the open plains or a Steenbok in rugged mountain terrain.

Many of the species in this book are known by several different common names, depending on region. For example, the Damara Dik-dik of Namibia is called Kirk's Dik-dik in East Africa. Until recently this was considered to be one widely separated species but is now known to be two distinct species. The Common Duiker is also known as Grimm's Duiker, the Crowned Duiker, Bush Duiker and Grey Duiker in different parts, although all refer to the same species *Sylvicapra grimmia*.

This is where scientific names are invaluable for identification as they do not vary according to region but are internationally recognized and so avoid confusion arising from regional variations and language differences.

MAJOR GAME RESERVES

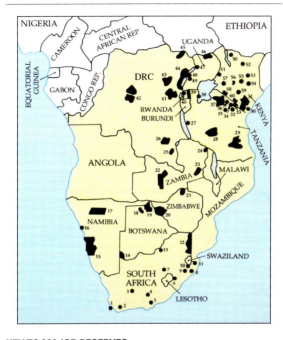

KEY TO MAJOR RESERVES

1. Table Mountain
2. Bontebok
3. Karoo
4. Mountain Zebra
5. Addo Elephant
6. uKhahlamba
7. Willem Pretorius
8. iSimangaliso
9. Hluhluwe-iMfolozi
10. uMkhuzi
11. Ndumo
12. Kruger
13. Pilanesberg
14. Kgalagadi
15. Namib-Naukluft
16. Cape Cross
17. Etosha
18. Moremi
19. Chobe
20. Hwange

21. Mana Pools
22. Kafue
23. South Luangwa
24. Nyika Plateau
25. Kundelungu
26. Upemba
27. Gombe Stream
28. Ruaha
29. Selous
30. Shimba Hills
31. Tsavo
32. Arusha
33. Mt Kilimanjaro
34. Kilimanjaro
35. Tarangire
36. Ngorongoro
37. Serengeti
38. Rubondo Island
39. Akagera
40. Volcanoes

41. Kahuzi-Biega
42. Salonga
43. Maiko
44. Virunga
45. Garamba
46. Kidepo
47. Murchison Falls
48. Semliki
49. Queen Elizabeth
50. East Turkana
51. Mt Elgon
52. Marsabit
53. Samburu
54. Meru
55. Mt Kenya
56. Aberdares
57. Lake Nakuru
58. Masai Mara
59. Nairobi
60. Amboseli

KEY TO SYMBOLS

Elephant (p.11)

Rhinos (p.12)

Hippo (p.14)

Buffalo (p.15)

Zebras (p.16)

Okapi (p.18)

Giraffe (p.19)

Antelope (p.20)

Warthog (p.62)

Bushpigs (p.63)

Aardvark (p.65)

Lion (p.66)

Leopard (p.68)

Cheetah (p.69)

Small Cats (p.70)

Civet (p.73)

Genets (p.74)

Hyaenas (p.76)
Aardwolf (p.79)

Wild Dog (p.80)

Jackals (p.81)
Foxes (p.84)

Otters (p.86)

Honey Badger (p.88)

Weasel (p.88)

Polecat (p.89)

Mongooses (p.90)

Suricate (p.95)

Seal (p.96)

Dugong (p.97)

Gorillas (p.98)

Chimpanzees (p.100)

Baboons (p.102)

Monkeys (p.104)

Bushbabies (p.110)

Pangolin (p.112)

Rabbits (p.113)

Hares (p.114)

Rock Hyrax (p.116)

Porcupine (p.117)

Springhare (p.118)

Molerat (p.119)

Squirrels (p.120)

Dormouse (p.121)

Gerbils (p.122)
Rats (p.124)

Dassie Rat (p.125)

Mice (p.126)

Elephant Shrews (Sengis) (p.130)

Shrews (p.132)

Golden Mole (p.134)

Hedgehog (p.135)

Bats (p.136)

SAVANNA ELEPHANT *Loxodonta africana* SH 2.5–3.4 m

FOREST ELEPHANT *Loxodonta cyclotis*

This, the largest land mammal, is so well known that it requires no detailed description. Cows have a mass of up to 3.5 tons and bulls 6.3 tons, and they are characterized by a long, mobile trunk, massive ears, and tusks. Tusks are absent in some cow populations; where present they continue to grow throughout life but are used for digging, probing for food and for fighting and, as a result, wear and suffer breakages, so never reach their full potential size. Elephant occur in a wide range of habitats, the only requirements being shade, water and ample food. Small herds, consisting of one dominant cow (matriarch), her young of different ages, and related cows and calves, are the common social grouping but several herds may come together for short periods. Adult bulls usually only join the family herds to mate with oestrus females, otherwise spending their time alone or in bachelor groups. Calves may be born at any time of the year, after a 22-month gestation period. The Elephant diet includes a very wide range of plants, which varies according to the season. Elephant numbers have declined drastically in recent years as a result of increased poaching and loss of habitat and today probably less than 500 000 remain in Africa.

Reserves: Addo Elephant; Hluhluwe-iMfolozi; Kruger; Pilanesberg; Etosha; Moremi; Chobe; Hwange; Mana Pools; Kafue; South Luangwa, Upemba; Ruaha; Tsavo; Arusha; Lake Manyara; Ngorongoro; Ruwenzori; Virunga, Garamba; Kidepo; Murchison Falls; Queen Elizabeth; Mt Elgon; Marsabit; Samburu; Mt Kenya, Aberdares; Masai Mara; Amboseli; Meru; Tarangire; Selous; Mukumi.

SQUARE-LIPPED (WHITE) RHINOCEROS
Ceratotherium simum SH 1.8 m

Square lip

This species once had a very wide distribution, wherever there was suitable habitat. Slaughtered for its horns, which are believed to have medicinal properties and are sought after by trophy hunters, it was brought to the brink of extinction. Today, thanks to intensive conservation efforts, especially in KwaZulu-Natal, it now occurs in many reserves and privately owned game farms in southern Africa. Unfortunately, this only applies to the subspecies, as *C.s.cottoni*, the northern form, occurred only in the Garamba National Park in Democratic Republic of Congo (DRC) but is now considered to be extinct. The White Rhinoceros is the *larger of the two* African species, with a mass of between 1.4 and 2.3 tons. Apart from size it can be distinguished from the following species by *the large, pointed ears, the broad, square muzzle and the prominent neck hump.* Being a grazer, this species shows a preference for areas with short grass and thickets. Dominant bulls form territories which they defend, in contrast to Hook-lipped Rhino males which do not defend territories. Animals are commonly seen together in groups, grazing in favoured pastures, or at mud wallows. Large dung middens are scattered within the home range and, as these are often close to roads, they are a common sight in reserves where the animals occur. A 40-kg calf is dropped after a gestation period of 16 months, and always walks in front of the mother.

Reserves: Hluhluwe-iMfolozi; uMkhuzi; Kruger; Pilanesberg; Chobe; Lake Nakuru.

HOOK-LIPPED (BLACK) RHINOCEROS *Diceros bicornis* SH 1.6 m

Hairy ears are a characteristic of this species

Also known as the Hook-lipped Rhinoceros, numbers of this magnificent animal are sligthly more than 5 000 despite poaching. The smaller (800–1 100 kg) of the two rhinoceros species in Africa, the Black Rhinoceros has a *comparatively short head, two horns on the front of the face and a pointed upper lip* – used to grasp twigs and shoots which are snapped off, or cut by the cheek-teeth. It requires areas with shrubs and trees from which to browse, and with dense thickets for cover. This species is usually solitary but groups may be seen at waterholes. During the day Black Rhinos lie up in dense cover and are rarely seen. Mating takes place at any time of the year and a single calf, with a mass of some 40 kg, is dropped after a gestation period of 15 months. The calf either runs alongside or behind the mother.

Reserves: Addo Elephant; Hluhluwe-iMfolozi; uMkhuzi; Kruger; Pilanesberg; Etosha; Hwange; Mana Pools; North Luangwa; Tsavo; Serengeti; Nairobi; Ngorongoro; Lake Nakuru; Masai Mara; Selous.

HIPPOPOTAMUS *Hippopotamus amphibius* SH 1.5 m

A large (1–2 tons), *semi-aquatic* mammal that is unmistakable with its barrel-like body, short, stocky legs, and *massive, broad-muzzled head*. The skin is greyish-black in colour with a pinkish tinge at the skin folds and around the eyes and ears. Its deep, *roaring grunts and snorts* are typical of many African waterways. During the day the Hippo spends most of its time in the water but it is also fond of basking on sandbanks, particularly during the cooler winter months. Herds of 10 to 15 animals, consisting of a dominant bull, and cows with their calves, are usual but larger groupings are not uncommon. At night they leave the water and follow fixed pathways to the grazing grounds. On land the dominant bulls mark their territories by vigorously flicking dung on to bushes and rocks with the short tail. Territories are pear-shaped, being narrow at the water but widening towards their grazing grounds. A 30-kg calf is born on land, amongst dense cover.

Reserves: iSimangaliso; Ndumo; Kruger; Moremi; Chobe; Mana Pools; Kafue; South Luangwa; Upemba; Tsavo; Arusha; Lake Manyara; Ngorongoro; Salonga; Ruwenzori; Virunga; Murchison Falls; Queen Elizabeth; Meru; Masai Mara; Samburu.

BUFFALO *Syncerus caffer* SH 1.4 m

Shaen Adey / IOA

Female Forest Buffalo

The only *wild cattle* occurring in Africa, Buffalo are *massive and heavily built* animals (♂700 kg). Adult bulls are dark brown to black in colour but cows are usually more brownish and calves are reddish-brown. The *large horns* are characteristic and when viewed from the front form a shallow 'W'. The hair-fringed ears hang below the horns. Buffalo show a preference for open woodland savanna, but an abundance of suitable grass, water and cover are essential. Depending on the size of the mixed herds there may be one or more dominant bulls. Bulls frequently form bachelor herds but solitary bulls are also common. Herds come to water in the early morning and late afternoon. Most calves are born during the rains, and are able to keep up with the herd just hours after the birth. A smaller subspecies, the Forest Buffalo (*Syncerus c. nanus*) occurs in the north-west. It is distinctive, being comparatively small and lightly built with a fairly *thick coat of reddish hair*. The horns are not as heavily formed as in the Buffalo and lack a 'boss'. The Forest Buffalo occurs in dense forests and their fringes, and some recognize it as a full species.

Reserves: Addo Elephant; Willem Pretorius; Hluhluwe-iMfolozi; Kruger; Moremi; Chobe; Hwange; Mana Pools; Kafue; South Luangwa; Upemba; Tsavo; Arusha; Serengeti; Ruwenzori; Virunga; Garamba; Kidepo; Murchison Falls; Queen Elizabeth; Mt Elgon; Marsabit; Samburu; Meru; Mt Kenya; Aberdares; Masai Mara; Nairobi; Amboseli; Lake Nakuru; Ruaha; Selous.

CAPE MOUNTAIN ZEBRA *Equus zebra zebra* SH 1.3–1.5 m

Two subspecies are recognized but they are very similar and can be separated according to distribution: Hartmann's (*E.z.hartmannae*) occurring naturally only in Namibia and the Cape Mountain Zebra only in the Western and Eastern Cape provinces. The Cape subspecies is white with black stripes and lacks the 'shadow stripes' of the Plains Zebra. The legs are striped to the hoof and on the upperside of the rump and tail there is a series of transverse black stripes forming a *'grid-iron' pattern* which is characteristic of this species only. This animal of mountainous terrain and of adjacent plateaux and plains is now restricted to conservation areas. It lives in small herds consisting of an adult stallion and several mares and their foals. A stallion may control a herd for up to 15 years until he is deposed by a younger stallion. Young stallions form bachelor herds. A single foal may be dropped at any time of year.

Reserves: Table Mountain; Bontebok; Karoo; Mountain Zebra; Camdeboo; Addo Elephant.

GREVY'S ZEBRA *Equus grevyi* SH 1.5 m

This zebra is characterized by its *narrow black stripes* on a white background, its *lack of 'shadow stripes'* and its white, unstriped underparts; a *broad, dark stripe runs along the spine.* The legs are densely striped and the ears are long, broad and rounded. A grazer, this species inhabits semi-desert plains and dry open woodland savanna. Stallions gather in bachelor herds, with mares and foals collecting in separate nursery herds, but on occasion they all gather in mixed herds. Territorial stallions protect their areas from other adult stallions but allow nursery herds to pass freely through them. Although drought may force stallions to abandon their territories, the males return with the onset of the rains. Herds move over large areas which makes conservation of this species more difficult. There has been a considerable decline in the number and range of this species in recent years. Births usually coincide with the onset of the rains.

Reserves: East Turkana; Samburu; Meru.

PLAINS ZEBRA *Equus burchellii/quagga* SH 1.3 m

Also known as Burchell's or Chapman's Zebra, this stocky animal is striped with black and white and, depending on the subspecies, may or may not have '*shadow stripes*' superimposed on the white stripes. There is, however, considerable variation in patterning. Stripes extend on to the underparts and there is a well-developed, erect black and white mane that extends from the head to the top of the shoulders. This is a species of open woodland and grassland. It associates in small family herds consisting of one stallion, mares and their foals. Unattached stallions join together in bachelor herds. Larger herds are formed on a temporary basis but the family herds maintain their unity. The characteristic barking call ('kwa-ha-ha') is frequently heard. Although they occasionally browse they feed mainly on grass. A single 30-kg foal may be dropped at any time of the year but the birth usually coincides with the rains.

Reserves: Hluhluwe-iMfolozi; uMkhuzi; Kruger; Pilanesberg; Etosha; Chobe; Hwange; Kafue; South Luangwa; Ruaha; Tsavo; Ngorongoro; Serengeti; Samburu; Nairobi; Amboseli; Masai Mara; Lake Nakuru.

OKAPI *Okapia johnstoni* SH 1.6 m

Rump markings

Only discovered at the beginning of the 20th century, the Okapi has an average mass of 230 kg and *superficially has a giraffe-like appearance but with a much shorter neck.* The short, velvety coat is rich chocolate-brown in colour and the hair has a distinct reddish or purplish gloss. The *upperparts of the legs and buttocks are conspicuously marked with black and white transverse stripes.* Short, hair-covered horns are carried by the male only. The Okapi is a solitary animal and is rarely seen in its dense forest habitat. It is predominantly diurnal with only limited nocturnal activity. Browse, easily retrieved by means of the very long tongue, makes up virtually all of its food intake. Okapi live singly or in small loosely associated groups. The Leopard is the principal predator. A single calf may be born at any time of the year.

Reserves: Salonga; Maiko; Virunga.

GIRAFFE *Giraffa camelopardalis* SH 2.0–3.5 m

Southern Giraffe

Reticulated Giraffe, Kenya

Being the tallest mammal in the world (up to 5.2 m) this species does not require detailed description. With its extremely long legs and neck it is instantly recognizable and is a common sight in many of the principal game parks. The beautiful lattice pattern of the coat consists of shaded patches separated by networks of light-coloured bands. Several subspecies are recognized, based on coat patterning. Those found in the area covered by this book, from north to south, are: the Nubian Giraffe (*G. c. camelopardalis*), Reticulated Giraffe (*G. c. reticulata*), Rothschild's or Baringo Giraffe (*G. c. rothschildi*), Kenyan Giraffe (*G. c. tippelkircht*) and the Southern Giraffe (*G. c. giraffa*). Although others have been described, it is unlikely that they are all valid because there is much variation between individuals. As they are browsers, Giraffes are restricted to areas of dry savanna woodland. Although they are usually seen in herds of four to 30 individuals, these groups are unstable and there is much movement between herds. Mature bulls associate only temporarily with cows. Because of their great height, Giraffe have access to food out of the range of other browsers. They use their lips to pull twigs into the mouth while the tongue curls around them and strips the leaves off. Calves, with a mass of about 100 kg at birth, are able to stand within the hour but join the herd only after two or three weeks. Widely introduced to game farms well outside their natural range in South Africa. Increasingly rare outside protected areas.

Reserves: Hluhluwe-iMfolozi; uMkhuzi; Kruger; Pilanesberg; Kgalagadi; Etosha; Moremi; Chobe; Hwange; South Luangwa; Tsavo; Arusha; Lake Manyara; Serengeti; Garamba; Kidepo; Murchison Falls; Marsabit; Samburu; Meru; Masai Mara; Nairobi; Amboseli; Lake Nakuru; Kilimanjaro.

GEMSBOK/ORYX *Oryx gazella/beisa* SH 1.2 m

Beisa Oryx (East African subspecies)

This large, heavily built antelope has a thick neck, *long, rapier-like horns in both sexes* and a *black, horse-like tail*. The overall body colour is greyish-fawn and the underparts are white. Black features prominently in the body markings: as *stripes along the flanks, as patches on the upper legs and rump,* and as *a stripe down the throat.* The lower legs are predominantly white. The *black and white facial markings* are very distinctive. The calves are plain fawn and lack body markings. This is a species of open, dry terrain, including open woodland, grass plains and sand-dunes. Although they will drink, surface water is not essential. Herds of up to 15 animals are common but much larger groups come together, particularly during the rains. Mixed herds may be observed, as well as nursery herds consisting only of calves and cows. Bulls holding territories will attempt to keep herds within their area and only they will mate with receptive cows. Because of the arid nature of the environment in which Gemsbok/Oryx live, they are nomadic and may move considerable distances in search of new grazing. Grasses form much of their food intake but they also dig out roots and eat wild fruits. Calves are born mostly during the rains.

Reserves: Kgalagadi; Namaque; Augrabies; Namib-Naukluft; Etosha; Hwange; Tsavo; Serengeti; Samburu; Meru.

ELAND *Taurotragus oryx* SH 1.5–1.7 m

Top: *Mixed herd,* Above: *Eland bull*

This is the *largest antelope* found in the area, adult bulls reaching 900 kg. Two forms are recognized, with those from Zambia northwards having more distinct white vertical body stripes. Eland have a somewhat cow-like appearance and are generally fawn or tawny in colour, although the hair on the neck and shoulders becomes blue-grey with age. Adult bulls have a *distinct neck dewlap* and develop a patch of fairly long, coarse hair on the forehead. Both sexes bear *straight horns* (c.60 cm) with a shallow spiral, although those of the bull are thicker and the spiral is more pronounced. Although found in a wide range of habitats, they prefer open, scrub-covered plains and woodland savanna. Herds usually consist of 25 to 60 individuals but larger groupings do occur, particularly during the rains. In some areas, such as the Kalahari, herds move over great distances. Eland are well known for their jumping abilities. Predominantly browsers, they will also occasionally eat grass and dig for roots and bulbs with the front hooves. Although calves are born throughout the year, there is a distinct peak during the rains.

Reserves: Mountain Zebra; Addo Elephant; UKhahlamba; Kruger; Pilanesberg; Kgalagadi; Etosha; Chobe; Hwange; Kafue; South Luangwa; Upemba; Ruaha; Tsavo; Arusha; Ngorongoro; Serengeti; Samburu; Meru; Masai Mara; Nairobi; Amboseli.

SABLE ANTELOPE *Hippotragus niger* SH 1.3 m

This magnificent antelope is easily recognized by its large size (230 kg), the *jet-black coat (in the bull) contrasting with the white underparts* and the heavily ridged, *back-curved horns*. Horns are carried by both sexes but those of the cow are less robust. Cows and young bulls are usually reddish-brown to dark brown in colour with white underparts, while the calves are pale reddish-brown. The *black and white facial markings* are conspicuous in both sexes, as is the mane, which extends from the top of the neck to just beyond the shoulders. The ears are not tufted as in the Roan. Sable are usually found in areas of dry, open woodland with medium to tall grass, and permanent water is essential. Herds usually number from 10 to 30 individuals and territorial bulls maintain territories that overlap those ranges occupied by cow/calf herds; a dominant cow leads the nursery herd. Younger bulls form bachelor herds. Although predominantly grazers, Sable will also browse. Calves are dropped during the rains and remain hidden until they are strong enough to stay with the herd.

Reserves: Kruger; Chobe; Hwange; Mana Pools; Kafue; South Luangwa; Kundelungu; Upemba; Ruaha; Selous; Shimba Hills.

ROAN ANTELOPE *Hippotragus equinus* SH 1.4 m

This is the second-largest (270 kg) antelope species in the area, after the Eland. It has a somewhat horse-like appearance with a general greyish-brown colouring, frequently showing a reddish tinge. The *black and white facial markings* are distinctive, as are the *long, narrow ears with tasseled tips*. A distinctive mane extends from between the ears to beyond the shoulders. Both the bull and cow carry the heavily ridged, swept-back and curved horns. The calf has a body colour of light to dark reddish-brown but the facial markings resemble those of the adult. Roan inhabit areas of open or lightly wooded grassland but avoid areas with only short grass, favouring medium length and long grasses for food. They usually live in small herds of five to 12 animals which are led by a mature bull. Each herd also has a dominant cow and she selects feeding and resting areas, while the bull mates with receptive cows and keeps competing bulls away. Young bulls form bachelor herds. There is no fixed breeding season and the cow gives birth in bush cover where the calf remains until it is about two weeks old. Severely depleted in most areas, with major population declines in South Africa's Kruger National Park. There are substantial populations on game farms in that country.

Reserves: Kruger; Pilanesberg; Chobe; Hwange; Mana Pools; Kafue; South Luangwa; Nyika Plateau; Upemba; Ruaha; Shimba Hills; Tarangire; Serengeti; Garamba; Kidepo; Masai Mara.

COMMON WATERBUCK *Kobus ellipsiprymnus* SH 1.3 m

The Waterbuck is a large, robust antelope with a shaggy, grey-brown coat and a very *distinctive white ring encircling the rump*. Hair around the nose, mouth and above the eyes is white, as is the band running from the throat to the base of each ear. Only the bull carries the long, heavily ridged, forward-swept horns. Although lighter in colour, calves resemble the cows. This species is always found in association with permanent water, in proximity to woodland, open grassland close to cover and reedbeds, and can often be detected by the very pungent smell that the animals give off. Young bulls form bachelor herds, while cows and calves move in herds of five to 10 individuals. The nursery herds may cross the territories of one or more adult bulls. Calves are dropped throughout the year but mostly in the rainy season.

Reserves: iSimangaliso; Hluhluwe-iMfolozi; uMkhuzi; Kruger; Pilanesberg; Mapungubwe; Moremi; Chobe; Hwange; Mana Pools; South Luangwa; Selous; Tsavo.

DEFASSA WATERBUCK *Kobus e. defassa* SH 1.3 m

The Defassa Waterbuck is very similar in appearance to the Common Waterbuck but is generally (though not in all regions) paler in body colour. In place of the white ring encircling the rump this waterbuck has a *broad white patch*. Habitat preferences and behaviour are identical to those of the Common Waterbuck.

Reserves: Kafue; Katavi; Ngorongoro; Nairobi; Lake Nakuru; Queen Elizabeth; Murchison Falls; Lake Mburo.

GREATER KUDU *Tragelaphus strepsiceros* SH 1.4 m

Top: *Bulls,* Above: *Cow*

A large antelope that is grey-brown with six to 10 *vertical white stripes* down the sides of the body. It has *large, rounded ears*, a bushy tail which is dark above and white below and, in the case of the *bull, distinctive long, spiral horns*. Calves resemble the cows. This is an antelope of various woodland associations but it may penetrate arid areas along watercourses. It forms small herds of three to 10 animals but larger groups do occur. Bulls may form bachelor groups or live alone, except during the breeding period when they join a group of cows and their young. In protected areas these animals are commonly seen during the day but in disturbed areas they are nocturnal. They are predominantly browsers and their ability to eat many different plant species has contributed to their increase in range in some areas. A single calf is usually dropped during the rainy season but births have been recorded at other times.

Reserves: Karoo; Addo Elephant; Hluhluwe-iMfolozi; uMkhuzi; Kruger; Etosha; Morerni; Chobe; Hwange; Mana Pools; Kafue; South Luangwa; Ruaha; Ngorongoro; Kidepo; Marsabit; Lake Bogoria.

LESSER KUDU *Ammelaphus imberbis* SH 1 m

Top: *Ram,* Above: *Ewe and ram*

Arguably the most attractive of all the medium-sized antelope. The ram is considerably larger (100 kg) than the ewe (62 kg) and only he carries the *long (75 cm), spiralled horns.* This species has a slender appearance and is overall greyish-brown with *up to 15 narrow, vertical, white stripes down the sides* of the body, and *two large, white patches on the neck.* The legs are orange-brown. The white underside of the tail is prominently displayed when the animal runs. The Lesser Kudu occupies areas dominated by acacia woodland and dense scrub, and is rarely encountered in open country. Animals have a fixed home range and are solitary, live in pairs or form small groups, the latter usually comprising ewes and their lambs. Most activity takes place at night and in the cooler daylight hours. The diet is made up of browse although they do graze selectively. Lambs are born throughout the year but there are birth peaks in certain areas.

Reserves: Ruaha; Tsavo; Tarangire; Kidepo; Meru.

NYALA *Tragelaphus (Nyala) angasii* SH 1–1.1 m

Top: *Ewes and lambs,* Above: *Ram*

 A handsome antelope that is larger than the Bushbuck but smaller than the Greater Kudu. Only the male carries the *slightly spiralled, white-tipped horns*, has slate-grey colouring and is much larger than the female. Males also have a *long mane of erectile hair along the back*, and a long fringe hanging from the throat to between the hindlegs. The lower part of the legs is yellow-brown and there are *eight to 14 vertical white stripes on the sides*. The female is yellow-brown to chestnut with *up to 18 vertical white stripes* on the sides, and lacks both the mane and the long, shaggy hair of the male. Both sexes have bushy tails which are white below. Fawns resemble the females. Nyala occur in dry savanna woodland but never far from water. They are commonly seen in small groups, usually comprising females and fawns but mixed groups and solitary rams are also common. The rams are not territorial but impressive displays with raised manes and stiff-legged gait serve to establish dominance. These animals are browsers but will take grass on occasion.

Reserves: Hluhluwe-iMfolozi; uMkhuzi; Ndumo; Kruger.

SITATUNGA *Tragelaphus spekei* SH 90 cm

Top: *Ram,* Above: *Ewe*

Several subspecies are recognized, based on coloration, with those in the north being more distinctly marked than the southern forms. Some authorities recognize the southern, central and East African populations as three distinct species. The adult rams of this secretive antelope are larger than the ewes and carry *horns similar to those of the Nyala. The hair is dark and shaggy.* Ewes are usually more distinctly marked than the males, with transverse stripes and spotting on the flanks. The *hoofs are very distinctive*, being long (to 15 cm) and are capable of spreading widely – an adaptation to their *swampy habitat.* The Sitatunga is restricted to the semi-aquatic environment associated with swamps and dense reedbeds and will swim readily. The common grouping consists of an adult ram with one or more ewes and their young, but solitary animals and groups of subadults are also seen. They are active during the day but lie up on trampled mats of reeds during the hottest hours. They feed principally on reeds and grass but will also browse. A single calf is born in the dry season after a 220-day gestation.

Reserves: Moremi; Chobe; Kafue; Salonga; Queen Elizabeth; Kasanka; Saiwa Swamp.

BUSHBUCK *Tragelaphus sylvaticus/scriptus* SH 75 cm

Top: *Ewe,* Above: *Ram*

A medium-sized (30–45 kg) antelope that varies considerably in colour and patterning according to region, from light to dark brown with only a limited number of light markings to bright chestnut with numerous white stripes and spots. Only the males carry the short, sharp horns. There are always *two white patches on the throat* and white markings on the legs, and a *dorsal crest*, raised only for display, extends down the back of the ram. This antelope occurs in a wide range of bush and forest habitats associated with water. It is usually solitary but pairs and loose groupings of ewes and lambs are not uncommon. Much of their activity takes place at night but diurnal activity may also take place. Bushbuck are browsers. Lambs remain hidden for the first four months of life.

Reserves: Addo Elephant; iSimangaliso; Hluhluwe-iMfolozi; Kruger; Moremi; Chobe; Mana Pools; Kafue; South Luangwa; Nyika Plateau; Upemba; Arusha; Lake Manyara; Ngorongoro; Ruwenzori; Virunga; Garamba; Queen Elizabeth; Mt Elgon; Marsabit; Samburu; Meru; Mt Kenya; Aberdares; Masai Mara; Nairobi.

BONGO *Tragelaphus (Boocercus) euryceros* SH 1.25 m

Top: *Cow*, Above: *Calf and cow*

The Bongo is a large (♂300 kg; ♀240 kg) *forest-dwelling antelope* with both sexes carrying *stout, shallowly spiralled horns*. The body is generally *bright chestnut-red with 10–16 narrow but distinct white stripes* extending transversely from the shoulders to the rump. The underparts are dark in colour and the forelimbs are distinctly patterned in black and white. This is a species of dense forest and, in parts of East Africa, even bamboo thickets in montane areas. Most adult bulls live solitary lives but the cows and calves live in nursery herds that apparently are not very stable. Outside of the breeding peaks, mixed groups come together on a temporary basis. Bongo browse on a wide range of plants. After a gestation period of 284 days a single calf is dropped.

Reserves: Salonga; Virunga; Garamba; Mt Kenya; Aberdares.

LECHWE *Kobus leche* SH 1 m

Top: *Red Lechwe,* Above left: *Red Lechwe male,* Above right: *Black Lechwe male*

A medium-sized antelope with *hindquarters noticeably higher than the shoulders.* Only the ram has long, strongly ridged, lyre-shaped horns. Several distinctly marked subspecies are recognized. The Red Lechwe from the south has bright chestnut-coloured upperparts, with white extending from the chin to the belly. *Conspicuous black stripes extend down the front of the forelegs,* and the tail has a tip of black hair. Lechwe are restricted to riverine floodplains and seasonal swamps and are rarely found more than 2 km from permanent water. They will feed readily in shallow water, and feed almost exclusively on semi-aquatic grasses. Herds usually do not exceed 30 individuals but larger groups may be formed. Mature rams defend territories through which nursery herds pass, and will mate with receptive females. Small bachelor herds move on the edge of those areas held by territorial males.

Reserves: Moremi; Chobe; Kafue; Bangweulu; Blue Lagoon; Lochinvar.

PUKU *Kobus vardonii* SH 80 cm

This medium-sized antelope has a general *body colour of golden-yellow with paler sides* and off-white underparts. The legs are uniform brown in colour and the tail is the same colour as the upper body. Only the *ram has the relatively short, stout, lyre-shaped and well-ringed horns*. The Puku only occurs in the narrow grassland strips immediately adjacent to rivers and marshes. Herds usually number from five to 30 individuals. Adult rams defend small territories for short periods, mating with nursery-herd ewes that are receptive. Nursery herds move across areas held by several territorial rams. This animal is exclusively a grazer. There is a dry-season peak in births.

Reserves: Chobe; Kafue; South Luangwa; Kasanka; Ruaha.

KOB *Kobus kob* SH 92 cm

Very *similar in size and appearance to the Puku*, and considered by some authorities to be the same species. The ram is a well-built animal, with a mass of up to 120 kg, a muscular neck and thick lyrate horns. Ewes are more lightly built and do not have horns. A number of subspecies are recognized based on pelage colour. Most animals in the area are reddish-brown with a *white throat patch*, white underparts and *distinctive black markings on the front of the legs*. Floodplains and gentle hill country are the principal habitats but a permanent water source is a requirement. Kob live in herds of 15 to 40 individuals with larger groups forming at certain times. Where there are high densities, adult rams defend a very small circular territory called a territorial ground (also known as a lek) (c.50 m in diameter), which may have as many as 15 territories abutting. Ewes enter the territories for mating and move freely between the rams. Non-territorial rams join nursery herds. The Kob is a grazer.

Reserves: Ruwenzori; Garamba; Kidepo; Murchison Falls; Semliki; Queen Elizabeth.

MOUNTAIN REEDBUCK *Redunca fulvorufula* SH 72 cm

Top: *Ewe,* Above: *Ram*

A small (30 kg) antelope with grey-fawn upperparts and white underparts. The *hair on the head and neck* usually has a *yellowish tinge.* The tail is bushy and is held vertically when the animal is alarmed, prominently displaying the white under-surface. Only the male carries the *short, ridged and forward-curved horns.* As the common name suggests, these antelope are restricted to mountainous and hill country, with scattered bush and grassy slopes, but water is essential.

Nursery herds comprising between two and six ewes and their lambs move over areas held throughout the year by territorial rams. Rams without territories may remain solitary or join up to form small bachelor groups. Activity is both nocturnal and diurnal but animals lie up during the heat of the day. Mountain Reedbuck are grazers. A single lamb is born under cover and remains hidden for two to three months before joining the group.

Reserves: Mountain Zebra; UKhahlamba; Kruger; Pilanesberg; Mt Kilimanjaro; Ngorongoro; Kidepo; Meru; Lake Nakuru; Nairobi.

SOUTHERN REEDBUCK *Redunca arundinum* SH 80–95 cm

Ram

Ewe

This is a medium-sized antelope with brown or greyish-brown upperparts and white underparts. The short but bushy tail is grey-brown above but white below. A vertical *black stripe is present on the front surface of the forelegs.* Only the ram carries the forward-curved and partially ridged horns.

Southern Reedbuck live in areas with tall grass and reedbeds in the vicinity of permanent water. The normal grouping consists of a pair with the ram defending the territory, but larger groups may be seen. They are active both at night and during the day, and their loud alarm whistles are characteristic of areas in which they occur. These antelope are grazers. The lambs remain hidden for about two months after birth.

Reserves: iSimangaliso; Hluhluwe-iMfolozi; Kruger; Moremi; Chobe; Hwange; Mana Pools; Kafue; South Luangwa; Ruaha; Selous.

BOHOR REEDBUCK *Redunca redunca* SH 70–90 cm

A somewhat smaller animal than the Southern Reedbuck with *yellowish to pale red-brown upperparts* and white underparts. The *forelegs are marked with black*, and the horns – carried by the male only – are stout, short and forward-hooked. These antelope are closely associated with river floodplains, reedbeds and flooded grassland. Up to five females may live within the breeding territory of a single male. Groups of more than 20 animals have been observed but such gatherings are usually in response to a particularly favourable food supply. Very high densities occur in prime habitat. These animals are grazers. Lambs remain under cover for up to two months.

Reserves: Serengeti; Ruwenzori; Kidepo; Queen Elizabeth; Lake Nakuru; Tarangire.

GREY RHEBOK *Pelea capreolus* SH 75 cm

Top: *Ram,* Above: *Ewes*

A small (20 kg) graceful animal with *thick, woolly grey hair on the upperparts* and white underparts. It runs with a 'rocking horse' motion, displaying the white under-surface of the tail. It has long, narrow ears and a *large, black nose* with a somewhat swollen appearance. Only the ram carries the thin, straight, upright horns. Although normally restricted to hilly or mountainous country, they have adapted well to the rolling wheatlands in the southern extent of their range. The normal group consists of a territorial ram, several ewes and their lambs. Although mainly browsers, they do graze on occasion.

Reserves: Bontebok; uKhahlamba; Karoo; Camdeboo; De Hoop; Mountain Zebra.

BLACK WILDEBEEST *Connochaetes gnou* SH 1.2 m

Also known as the White-tailed Gnu, this antelope is somewhat grotesque with an *overall black appearance* and a *white, horse-like tail*. Both sexes have horns that bend steeply downwards, forwards and upwards. Bulls have a heavy 'boss' where the horns meet at the top of the head. The *face is covered in a brush-like tuft of hairs* which point outwards, and there is long hair on the throat and between the forelegs, extending onto the chest. An erect mane runs from the top of the neck on to the shoulders. This is a species of open scrub and grassland. Herds of cows and their young wander freely over the territories of bulls, and during the rut the bulls attempt to keep these herds within their control. Non-territorial bulls form bachelor herds. Herds are mainly active during the cooler daylight hours, lying up during the hot midday, although they do not seek shade. Black Wildebeest eat mostly grasses but they do browse occasionally too. Most calves are born during the mid-summer months. This antelope once occurred in great herds, usually in association with the now extinct Quagga, but was almost eradicated by hunters and farmers. Once one of the rarest large mammals in the world but now there are over 20 000 animals, the bulk of which are located in the Free State and adjoining areas of the Northern Cape, North-West and Gauteng. Large numbers of this wildebeest also occur in Namibia, far outside their natural range. Although it is illegal, some game farmers (and provincial authorities) have run this species and the Blue Wildebeest together, resulting in hybrid populations.

Reserves: Karoo; Mountain Zebra; UKhahlamba; Willem Pretorius; Golden Gate Highlands; Camdeboo.

BLUE WILDEBEEST *Connochaetes taurinus* SH 1.4 m

The *forequarters* of this large antelope *are higher and more robust than the hindquarters* and the head is large with a broad snout. Overall body colour is dark grey with a brown to bluish sheen and several *darker, vertical stripes* are present *from the neck to the front of the hindquarters*; hence the alternative name of Brindled (brown-streaked) Gnu for this species. A mane of longish, black hair extends down the back of the neck on to the shoulders, and a beard of black hair grows from the throat. Populations in the north-east are generally paler in colour and the beard is dirty white. Both sexes have horns, superficially similar to the Buffalo's, although those of the bull are more robust than the female's. The tail is black and horse-like. Calves are rufous-fawn in colour with a darker face. The Blue Wildebeest is an antelope of open grassland and savanna woodland. Herds of up to 30 individuals are typical although much larger temporary groupings are common in some areas; smaller herd units maintain their identity during these temporary congregations, however. Territorial bulls control 'mobile' territories in which they hold up to 150 cows and their young while on the move. However, nursery herds may move through the territories of several bulls and cows mate with more than one bull. Outside the mating season the cow herds are not herded by territorial bulls and move unhindered. Blue Wildebeest are grazers.

Reserves: Hluhluwe-iMfolozi; uMkhuzi; Kruger; Kgalagadi; Etosha; Moremi; Chobe; Hwange; Kafue; South Luangwa; Selous; Tarangire; Ngorongoro; Serengeti; Masai Mara; Nairobi; Amboseli.

LICHTENSTEIN'S HARTEBEEST
Alcelaphus lichtensteinii SH 1.25 m

Although a somewhat clumsy looking antelope with the *shoulders higher off the ground than the rump*, it is in fact a very agile, fast runner. The overall body colour is tawny-yellow with a slightly *darker 'saddle'* extending from the shoulders to the rump. The underparts are lighter in colour and there is an off-white patch on the rump. The tail is covered with long, black hair except at the base, which is white. Both sexes have horns with a 'Z'-shaped curvature and which are flattened at the base. These animals occupy open savanna woodland adjacent to marshes or floodplains. Herds of up to 10 are common although larger groups do congregate occasionally. A territorial bull resides with a number of cows and calves in a fixed home range, and bachelor herds live on the fringes of these areas. These hartebeest are predominantly grazers, feeding on taller grasses. After a gestation period of 240 days a single calf weighing about 15 kg is dropped, usually between July and October although the breeding season varies between regions. Although still a widespread species most populations are now scattered and isolated, with only small numbers occurring in southern Africa. The only animals found in South Africa are those introduced to the Kruger National Park from Malawi in the mid-1980s.

Reserves: Kruger; Kafue; South Luangwa; Upemba; Ruaha.

HUNTER'S HARTEBEEST *Damaliscus hunteri* SH 98 cm

Ardea London Ltd - Kenneth W. Fink

One of East Africa's rarer antelopes, this species has the same general appearance as the other hartebeests but is not as heavily built. It is uniformly tawny-yellow in colour with a white chevron between the eyes, and has a long, partly white tail. The horns do not resemble those of other hartebeests, lacking the typically broad 'boss', and superficially are more like those of the Impala. Hunter's Hartebeest is a species of open grassland and scattered scrub country in a very limited area. It congregates in herds of up to 25 individuals. Hunter's Hartebeest is also kown by the name Hirola.

Reserves: Tsavo East.

RED (BUBAL) HARTEBEEST *Alcelaphus buselaphus* SH 1.2 m

Top: *Red Hartebeest,*
Above: *Coke's Hartebeest*

Several subspecies (some authorities believe the subspecies should be recognized as full species) of this animal are recognized, based mainly on horn form and, to a lesser extent, on body colour. Only one subspecies occurs in the south. This high-shouldered, *low-rumped* antelope has a general body colour of fawn to golden-brown with *black markings on the front of a long face* and on all four legs. There is a well-defined, pale yellow or off-white patch on the rump. The shape of the horns is characteristic, ruling out confusion with other species. The Red Hartebeest lives in open savanna and lightly wooded country. Herd size is variable from 20 to many hundreds of individuals. Harem herds, consisting of a territorial bull, cows and their young, occupy the best grazing areas while bachelor herds feed on the fringe zones. The herds are subject to considerable movement and will cover great distances in search of fresh grazing. Most calves are born at the beginning of the rains.

Reserves: Karoo; Mountain Zebra; Addo Elephant; Kgalagadi; Etosha; Hwange; Selous; Tsavo; Serengeti; Kidepo; Masai Mara; Nairobi; Hell's Gate.

TSESSEBE *Damaliscus lunatus* SH 1.2 m

With its long face and its shoulders higher than the rump, this antelope could be mistaken for a hartebeest. The upperparts are dark reddish-brown with a *purplish sheen* but the upper legs, lower shoulder and head are somewhat darker in colour. The lower legs are brownish-yellow. Both sexes carry the heavily ringed, lyrate horns. Tsessebe are grazers and favour open savanna woodland with adjacent grassland where they show a preference for medium-high grasses, but particularly new grass on burnt areas. Herds are usually small, numbering up to six individuals, and are controlled by a territorial bull. Each herd lives permanently in a territory. Young bulls, driven away by harem bulls, form bachelor groups. In the south lambs are born from October to December.

Reserves: Pilanesberg; Kruger; Etosha; Moremi; Chobe; Hwange; Bangweulu.

TOPI (TIANG; KORRIGUM) *Damaliscus korrigum* SH 1.2 m

A fairly large antelope very similar to the Tsessebe and in fact classified by some authorities as the same species. *The shoulder is higher than the rump* and the overall body colour is reddish-brown to purplish-red with a *distinct sheen*. The lower part of the legs is orange-fawn. The horns are thick, deeply ringed and lyrate. Several different races are recognized. Topi inhabit open savanna woodland. Herds usually consist of between 15 and 30 animals but larger groupings are not unusual. They are often seen in the company of other herding animals, such as Blue Wildebeest and Plains Zebra. During the rut adult bulls establish territories, with nursery herds moving freely across them. Topi are grazers, favouring short grasses.

Reserves: Tsavo; Serengeti; Masai Mara.

BLESBOK *Damaliscus pygargus phillipsi* SH 95 cm

The Blesbok can be separated from the Bontebok by its reddish-brown coat, which *lacks a purple gloss* and by the rump, which is not white. The *white facial blaze* is usually *broken by a brown band between the eyes*. In general appearance the horns of this subspecies are similar to the Bontebok but the *upper surface is straw-coloured*. An animal of the open grassland, it does not have a fixed home range throughout the year as the Bontebok does, and in winter large mixed herds are formed. Lambs are born between November and January. The Blesbok is one of the most important commercial game species in South Africa, along with the Springbok.

Reserves: Mountain Zebra; Willem Pretorius; Golden Gate Highlands; Camdeboo.

BONTEBOK *Damaliscus pygargus dorcas* SH 90 cm

Top: *Ram*, Above: *Lamb*

A handsome antelope, with its rich dark brown coat, darker sides and upper limbs, and sharply contrasting white underparts, buttocks and lower limbs. A purple gloss on the upperparts is most noticeable in adult rams. An unbroken white blaze extends from between the horns to the muzzle, only narrowing between the eyes. These antelope stand higher at the shoulders than at the rump and the head is long and pointed.

Both sexes carry simple, lyre-shaped horns, which are black in colour and heavily ringed. Bontebok occur naturally in the extreme south-west only. Territorial rams hold permanent areas through which nursery herds are free to wander, except during the rut from January to March when the rams attempt to keep the herds in their territories for mating. Lambs are born in September and October.

Reserves: Table Mountain; Bontebok; De Hoop.

IMPALA *Aepyceros melampus* SH 90 cm

Black-faced Impala ewe

This medium-sized (40–50 kg) antelope is a common sight in many of the major game parks. The upperparts are reddish-fawn, becoming paler on the sides, and the chest, belly, throat and chin are white. Each *buttock has a vertical black stripe. Above the hoof* of each hindleg is a *tuft of black hair,* which is unique to this species. Only the rams carry the long, graceful, lyrate horns. In northern Namibia and south-west Angola the subspecies known as the Black-faced Impala is distinguished by its distinct black facial blaze. Impala favour open savanna woodland and avoid open grassland. In the south, dominant rams are only territorial during the January to May rut, spending the rest of the year in bachelor herds. During the rut rams typically give vent to a *range of growls, snorts and roars.* The home range of a nursery herd may overlap the territories of several rams which attempt to hold groups of 15 to 20 ewes for mating. Impala browse and graze.

Reserves: Hluhluwe-iMfolozi; uMkhuzi; Kruger; Etosha; Chobe; Hwange; Mana Pools; Kafue; South Luangwa; Ruaha; Lake Manyara; Ngorongoro; Samburu; Meru; Nairobi; Tsavo.

GERENUK *Litocranius walleri* SH 95 cm

With its *very long, slender neck and long legs*, this gazelle is unmistakable. The upperparts are rufous-fawn, the sides are paler and the underparts are white and clearly separated by a dark line. There is a *white ring around the eye that extends as a line towards the snout*. Only the ram carries horns, these being fairly short (30 cm), heavily ringed and distinctive in form. This is a species of arid country, usually in association with thorn scrub. The Gerenuk is predominantly a solitary animal but small groups are not uncommon. Its long legs and neck enable it to browse at heights inaccessible to other species. These animals frequently increase this advantage by standing on their hindlegs.

Reserves: Tsavo; Samburu; Meru.

SPRINGBOK *Antidorcas marsupialis* SH 75 cm

Top: *Ram,* Above: *Ewes*

The Springbok is the only gazelle in southern Africa and it is distinctly marked. A dark *red-brown stripe* separates the fawn-brown upperparts from the white underparts. The *head is white* with a thin stripe running from each eye to the corner of the upper lip. A *long-haired dorsal crest* is visible only when the animal 'pronks': a stiff-legged jump with back arched. Both sexes have heavily ringed, lyre-shaped horns but those of the ewe are much thinner. Springbok live on the arid, open plains of the interior. During the rut rams hold and defend temporary territories in which they herd ewe groups. Herds are usually small but large numbers may be seen together, particularly at favoured feeding grounds. Many herds are mixed but bachelor herds are also common. Springbok are mixed feeders and they will also dig for roots and bulbs with their hooves. Lambs are usually born during the summer rainy season.

Reserves: Karoo; Namaqua; Mountain Zebra; Willem Pretorius; Kgalagadi; Namib-Naukluft; Etosha; Camdeboo; Nxai Pan.

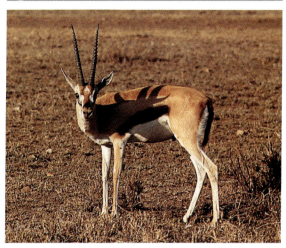

THOMSON'S GAZELLE *Eudorcas thomsoni* SH 65 cm

A *small gazelle* that rarely has a mass of more than 28 kg. The upper body colour is generally a pale yellowish-fawn with a *broad black lateral stripe* clearly separating it from the white underparts. There is a *distinct white eye-ring*, and the *short tail is completely covered with black hair*. The horns grow fairly close together, are strongly ringed and average 30 cm in length, although those of the ewe are more slender and usually shorter than the male's. This species occupies open grassland and avoids dense bush.

Commonly called 'Tommies', these antelope form small herds of up to 60 individuals, which are led by an old female, and accompanied by a single mature male. At certain times of the year many herds amalgamate when moving to favoured feeding grounds. This is one of the most abundant antelope species in East Africa. Thomson's Gazelle is commonly found in association with Grant's Gazelle and with Impala. It is predominantly a grazer, with browse forming only a small part of its diet. Lambs may be dropped at any time of the year but there is a peak in births towards the end of the rains.

Reserves: Ngorongoro; Serengeti; Masai Mara; Nairobi; Amboseli; Lake Nakuru.

GRANT'S GAZELLE *Nanger granti* SH 82 cm

This *large gazelle* (up to 80 kg) with *uniformly fawn upperparts* and white underparts could be mistaken for the Impala ram or for Thomson's Gazelle. The *inner buttocks are white with a black vertical streak at the outer edge*, and a lateral line is present although this is rather faint in adults. A *white facial stripe passes from the eye to the muzzle.* The long, well-ridged horns vary considerably in spread according to race. This species has a wide habitat tolerance, ranging from semi-desert scrub to open savanna woodland, but avoids long grass. Unlike wildebeest and Thomson's Gazelles, this antelope does not undertake seasonal migrations. They are mixed feeders, taking both grass and browse. Herds of up to 30 individuals are formed, an adult ram controlling a group of ewes and their offspring. Grant's Gazelle breeds at any time of the year. Several subspecies of this antelope are recognized, the form of the horns being the principal distinguishing factor. For example, *petersi* has relatively short, nearly straight and narrow horns, whereas *robertsi* has widely diverging horns with the tips pointing downwards.

Reserves: Ngorongoro; Serengeti; Samburu; Masai Mara; Nairobi; Amboseli; Meru; Tsavo; Ruaha.

KLIPSPRINGER *Oreotragus oreotragus* SH 60 cm

Top: *Ram,* Above: *Ewe*

Both the appearance and habitat of this small (10–13 kg) antelope help to separate it from other species. The *coarse, spiky hair* varies in colour from yellow-brown to grey-yellow, and has a distinctly grizzled appearance. White to creamy hair is present on the underparts, chin and lips. This is the only antelope that *walks on the tips of its hoofs*. The ram bears short, vertical horns which are widely separated at the base, and in some northern populations the ewe also has horns. Klipspringer only occur on mountain ranges and other rocky habitats. They are extremely agile and nimble even over the roughest terrain. They live in pairs or in small family parties, and adult rams are territorial. Groups use communal dung heaps scattered throughout the home range. The loud, nasal alarm whistles are often the first sign of the animals' presence. This species gets most of its food from browse. A single lamb, with a mass of about 1 kg, may be dropped at any time of the year.

Reserves: Karoo; Mountain Zebra; UKhahlamba; Kruger; Namib-Naukluft; Hwange; Upemba; Tsavo; Lake Manyara; Ngorongoro; Serengeti; Mt Kilimanjaro; Samburu.

ORIBI *Ourebia ourebi* SH 60 cm

Top: *Ewe,* Above: *Ram*

The largest (14 kg) of the small antelope, it could be mistaken for a Steenbok from a distance. The upperparts are rufous yellow-orange, the underparts are white and there is a pale throat patch. It has a *relatively long neck*, smaller ears than the Steenbok and a distinctive *tail which is short and has a black tip*. The ram has short, erect, partly ridged horns. Oribi occur only in open, short grassland with taller grass patches to provide cover. The strongly territorial ram may be accompanied by as many as four ewes. Communal dung heaps serve to demarcate the territory. When disturbed they give a sharp whistle and run off rapidly for a short distance but then turn and watch the source of the disturbance. Because of this habit, Oribi are highly vulnerable to poachers using dogs. In some areas this has resulted in local extinctions and major population declines. Occasional stiff-legged jumps and the display of the black-tipped tail when alarmed are diagnostic. They feed on selected short grasses. The single lamb is born during the summer months and remains hidden for the first four months.

Reserves: UKhahlamba; Chobe; Kafue; South Luangwa; Upemba; Serengeti; Akagera; Kidepo; Murchison Falls; Mt Elgon; Masai Mara; Lake Mburo; Addo Elephant.

STEENBOK *Raphicerus campestris* SH 50 cm

Top: *Ram,* Above: *Ewe*

One of the most widely distributed of the so-called dwarf antelope and the one most frequently seen. The *large ears* are distinctive. There are no characteristic markings and much of the body is covered with rufous-fawn hair but the underparts and insides of the legs are white. The rufous-fawn tail is very short. The ram has short, sharp-pointed, vertical horns. Steenbok show a preference for open areas where there is some cover. They are territorial and live singly or in pairs. They are unique among antelope in that they defecate and urinate in shallow scrapes which are dug by the front hoofs and then covered again. The Steenbok is a mixed feeder. A single 900-g lamb is usually born during the summer.

Reserves: Bontebok; Karoo; Mountain Zebra; Willem Pretorius; Hluhluwe-iMfolozi; uMkhuzi; Kruger; Pilanesberg; Kgalagadi; Namib-Naukluft; Etosha; Chobe; Hwange; Ngorongoro; Serengeti; Nairobi.

SHARPE'S GRYSBOK *Raphicerus sharpei* SH 50 cm

Top and above: *Ewes*

Very similar in appearance to the Cape Grysbok but the ranges of the two do not overlap. The upperparts are not as richly red in colour and it is smaller (7.5 kg) than the Cape Grysbok. Low thicket, often in association with vegetated rocky hills, and adjacent areas of open grass are favoured habitat, as well as dry, riverine woodland with adequate scrub cover. Although they are mainly nocturnal, the nature of their habitat may cause activity during the cooler hours of the day to be overlooked. Sharpe's Grysbok is predominantly a browser but will also eat grass. Rams are believed to defend a territory and it is likely that a pair lives in loose association within a home range. Available information indicates that lambs may be born at any time of the year.

Reserves: Kruger; Hwange; Mana Pools; Kafue; South Luangwa; Selous.

CAPE GRYSBOK *Raphicerus melanotis* SH 54 cm

Top: *Ewe,* Above left and right: *Rams*

A small (10 kg), squat antelope with rufous-brown *upperparts* liberally *flecked with white hairs*. The underparts are lighter brown and are not flecked. The *tail is very short* and hardly visible, and the ears are quite large with white hairs lining the inner surface. The ram has short, smooth, slightly back-angled horns. The Cape Grysbok is confined to the southern tip of Africa where it is closely associated with fairly dense bush cover. It is predominantly nocturnal and solitary, and is a mixed feeder, taking grasses, herbs and leaves. A single lamb is dropped at any time of the year

Reserves: Table Mountain; Bontebok; Addo Elephant; West Coast; Namaqua; Garden Route.

RED DUIKER *Cephalophus natalensis* SH 43 cm

John Carlyon

A small (14 kg) antelope that has *rich reddish-brown hair* with paler colouring on the chin and throat. The short *tail* is distinctly *tipped with black and white hairs* and *a crest is located on top of the head*. Both sexes have the very short, backward-pointing horns. This duiker inhabits forest and dense woodland, and usually occurs singly or in pairs, which may live in loose association within the same home range. The tiny, currant-sized dung pellets are deposited in small heaps in specific areas. Lambs have been recorded throughout the year.

Reserves: iSimangaliso; Ndumo; Kruger; Mt Kenya; Selous; Kilimanjaro; Tsavo; Akagera.

BLUE DUIKER *Philantomba monticola* SH 35 cm

With a mass of 4 kg, this is the *smallest antelope* in the area. The upperparts vary from slate-grey to dark brown *with a grey-blue sheen*, and the underparts are white to off-white. The short, bushy black and white tail is almost constantly wagging. Both sexes have very short, spiky horns that are often hidden in the head crest. Forest and dense bush are essential to this antelope but it will often feed in open glades. Because of the dense nature of its habitat and its timid nature the Blue Duiker is seldom seen. The small heaps of tiny dung pellets and tiny (20 mm) tracks in the mud are often the only signs of their presence. They make use of regular pathways within the home range, and are solitary or live in loosely associated pairs. Blue Duikers are active both at night and during the day. A single 400-g lamb may be born in any month.

Reserves: iSimangaliso; Ndumo; Kafue; South Luangwa; Upemba; Garamba; Mt Elgon.

YELLOW-BACKED DUIKER *Cephalophus sylvicultor* SH 78 cm

The *largest of all the duikers*, weighing as much as 80 kg, this species is overall dark greyish-brown with a very *distinct yellowish-brown patch covering much of the lower back* but broader at the rump than at the shoulders. This animal occupies various forest associations but also utilizes the fringes of these densely wooded areas. In common with other duiker species, it is a solitary forager and makes regular use of the same pathways. Wild fruits, berries and fungi make up the bulk of its diet but it will also feed on a wide array of plants.

Reserves: Kafue; Upemba; Salonga; Virunga.

BAY DUIKER *Cephalophus dorsalis* SH 56 cm

Laila Bahaa-el-din

This is a heavily built (24 kg) forest duiker, reddish in colour, with dark brown to black legs and a *black midline down the back and the belly*. It inhabits mixed forest, thickets and their margins. Fruits make up much of the diet but birds and other animal foods may be taken.

Reserves: Salonga, Virunga, Maiko.

COMMON (GRIMM'S) DUIKER *Sylvicapra grimmia* SH 50 cm

Top: *Ewe,* Above: *Ram*

This is a large (20 kg) duiker that has uniform grey-brown to reddish-yellow upper parts and pale to white underparts. *Dark brown to black markings are present as a facial blaze and on the front surfaces of the forelegs*, and there is a small crest of *long hair between the horns*. The ram has short, heavily ringed horns. Unlike the forest duikers that walk with an arched back, this species *walks with a straight back*. It has a very wide habitat tolerance but shows a preference for scrub and lightly bushed areas, often close to human settlements. Common Duikers are solitary animals and appear to have evenly spaced territories which are marked with small, loose accumulations of dung. In some areas territories are small and densities may be very high. Activity takes place at night and during the cooler daylight hours. Principally browsers, they will also eat grass. A single 1.6-kg lamb is dropped at any time of year.

Reserves: Table Mountain; Bontebok; Karoo; Addo Elephant; Hluhluwe-iMfolozi; uMkhuzi; Kruger; Etosha; Chobe; Hwange; Mana Pools; Kafue; Upemba; Salonga; Virunga; Serengeti; Nairobi.

DAMARA DIK-DIK *Madoqua damarensis* SH 38 cm

M. kirkii
M. damarensis

There are five species of Dik-dik, this species occurring in south-western Africa. The very similar Kirk's Dik-dik (*M. kirkii*) occurs in eastern Africa. The Damara Dik-dik is a tiny (5 kg) antelope which is easily overlooked in the bush. It has an *elongated and very mobile nose* and a *tuft of long hair on the forehead* which is erected during certain social interactions. The upperparts are yellowish-grey with a grizzled appearance but the neck is paler than the shoulders and flanks. The underparts are either white or off-white and the large eyes are white-ringed. Only the rams have the short, spike-like horns which slope backwards. This Dik-dik inhabits fairly dense, dry woodland, often in association with rocky hillsides. It is normally seen singly, in pairs or in small family parties consisting of a ram, a ewe and her youngster. Rams are territorial and pairs use communal dung heaps within the home range. Dik-dik are mainly browsers and, apart from leaves, they eat fruits, seedpods and flowers. A single lamb of about 690 g is born during the summer months.

Reserves: Damara – Etosha; Kirk's – Ruaha; Ngorongoro; Serengeti; Masai Mara; Sarnburu; Meru; Tsavo.

SUNI *Neotragus moschatus* SH 35 cm

The Suni is a secretive antelope that is seldom seen. Although smaller (5 kg) than Sharpe's Grysbok, its *rich rufous-brown upperparts flecked with white hairs*, and white underparts could lead to confusion with that species. The *white-tipped tail is constantly flicking* from side to side. The *ears are pink-lined and give the appearance of being translucent.* Only the rams have the short, straight, heavily ringed horns, and there is a prominent gland in front of each of the ram's eyes. Suni are restricted to dry thickets and riverine woodland with dense undergrowth, and are mostly active at night and in the cooler daylight hours. An adult Suni ram is usually accompanied by one to four ewes in a fixed territory. Their habit of following fixed trails makes them vulnerable to snaring but densities remain high in many areas. A single fawn is born in the summer.

Reserves: iSimangaliso; uMkhuzi; Kruger; Mana Pools; Selous; Arusha; Mt Kilimanjaro; Mt Kenya; Amboseli.

WARTHOG *Phacochoerus africanus* SH 65 cm

This is one of four pig species occurring in the area covered by this book. The body is usually grey but takes on the colour of the local mud in which the animal frequently wallows. A *crest of long, erectile hair* extends down the full length of the back and is raised when the animal is under stress. The snout is typically pig-like and the canine teeth develop into *long, curved tusks,* most noticeable in boars. The *tail,* with its tuft of black hairs, is *held erect* when the Warthog runs. This is an animal of savanna and open woodland and is most active during the day. Groups or 'sounders' usually consist of sows and their piglets, or of single males. Warthog make use of abandoned Aardvark and Porcupine burrows but occasionally will dig their own. They are predominantly grazers and frequently kneel when feeding. Most births take place in the summer months.

Reserves: Hluhluwe-iMfolozi; uMkhuzi; Kruger; Pilanesberg; Etosha; Chobe; Hwange; Mana Pools; Kafue; South Luangwa; Upemba; Tsavo; Arusha; Mt Kilimanjaro; Lake Manyara; Ngorongoro; Serengeti; Virunga; Garamba; Queen Elizabeth; Marsabit; Meru; Samburu; Aberdares; Masai Mara; Nairobi; Amboseli; Lake Nakuru.

BUSHPIG *Potamochoerus larvatus* SH 55–88 cm

RED RIVER HOG *Potamochoerus porcus*

Top: *Bushpig,* Above: *Red River Hog*

The Bushpig has a typical pig-like appearance, a well-haired body, *tufts of hair at the tips of the ears*, and a long head. Colouring varies from region to region but is usually a shade of grey-brown. Piglets are dark brown and distinctly marked with pale stripes. The form known as the Red River Hog, occurring in the north-central region, is considered to be a distinct species. When it runs, it *holds its tail vertically downwards.* This pig is found only in areas of forest, dense bush, riverine woodland and reedbeds but will emerge at night to feed in more open areas. It is mostly active during the night but in undisturbed areas will also forage during the cooler morning and late afternoon hours. A group or 'sounder' is usually made up of four to 10 individuals – a dominant boar, a dominant sow, and other sows and their young; solitary animals and bachelor groups may be encountered. Both species are omnivorous.

Reserves: Addo Elephant; iSimangaliso; Hluhluwe-iMfolozi; uMkhuzi; Kruger; Chobe; Hwange; Mana Pools; Kafue; South Luangwa; Upemba; Arusha; Ngorongoro; Serengeti; Virunga; Garamba; Queen Elizabeth; Masai Mara; Mount Kenya.

GIANT FOREST HOG *Hylochoerus meinertzhageni* SH 96 cm

Roland van Bocstaele

By far the *largest wild pig* in the world, the males have an average mass of 235 kg while sows are somewhat smaller. They are *powerfully built* and are covered with coarse, black hair. The *muzzle is broad and flat*, the snout large, and tusks, particularly in the boar, are well developed. This species is closely associated with dense forest and also montane areas but will feed in adjacent open areas and clearings. It is estimated that home ranges average 10 km² but this varies according to the quality of food in an area. A social unit usually consists of a sow and her offspring of different ages, accompanied by a boar. Sounders may feed in close proximity to one another but boars are wary of each other and keep their distance. These pigs are predominantly grazers. Although young may be born at any time of the year, there may be birth peaks. The number of piglets born ranges from two to 11.

Reserves: Ruwenzori; Virunga; Garamba; Queen Elizabeth; Mt Elgon; Mt Kenya; Aberdares.

AARDVARK *Orycteropus afer* TL 1.4–1.8 m

Resembling no other mammal in our area, the Aardvark has a *long, pig-like snout, elongated tubular ears, a heavily muscled kangaroo-like tail,* an arched back, and stocky legs which end in spade-like nails. It has poor eyesight but its senses of smell and hearing are well developed. There is a sparse covering of coarse hair, and the skin colour is grey-fawn but is influenced by the soil colour of the area. This is one of the few species that has benefited from overgrazing and trampling by domestic stock. By trampling the grass, the stock make it more accessible to the termites upon which the Aardvark feeds. A species of wide habitat tolerance, it shows a preference for open woodland, sparse scrub and grassland. This strange animal is almost exclusively nocturnal, spending the day in large, self-excavated burrows. The males are much more nomadic than the females. During their search for the ants and termites that make up their diet, they may cover considerable distances each night. The holes that they excavate at the base of termite mounds are a sure sign of their presence. The single young, born during the rainy season, has a mass of 2 kg at birth (adults 40–70 kg) and it begins to follow the mother when it is about three weeks old.

Reserves: Karoo; Mountain Zebra; Camdeboo; Addo Elephant; Hluhluwe-iMfolozi; Kruger; Kgalagadi; Etosha; Chobe; Hwange; Mana Pools; Kafue; South Luangwa; Upemba; Tsavo; Ngorongoro; Serengeti; Virunga; Garamba; Queen Elizabeth; Nairobi.

CARNIVORES Order Carnivora

Some 48 species of carnivore occur within the area, including six canids, three hyaenas, eight cats, three otters and a broad range of genets and mongooses.

LION *Panthera leo* SH ♂1.2 m, ♀1.0 m

Top: *Lion*, Above: *Lioness and lion*

The lion is the largest of the African cats, males reaching up to 225 kg, although females rarely exceed 150 kg. The *male has a mane of long hair* that extends from the sides of the face to the shoulders and chest. The mane colour is variable, from pale tawny (blond) to black, and the overall body colour is usually reddish-grey to tawny; cubs have faint spotting on the sides. The *long, short-haired tail has a dark tip.* Previously found throughout the area in most habitats except forest, the lion has been eradicated from much of its former range. It is the most social of all cat species, forming prides that may contain from three to 30 individuals, depending on the area and prey availability. A pride consists of one or more adult males, several adult females and cubs. Males and females in each pride defend a territory against other lions, although some prides are nomadic. Territories are marked with urine, droppings and also by the mighty roars that carry for considerable distances. During the heat of the day lions lie up in the shade, doing most of their hunting at night or during the cooler morning hours. Female members do most of the hunting but the males feed first at a kill. Medium- to large-sized mammal prey forms the bulk of their diet, but lion will also scavenge. Cubs may be born at any time of the year in litters of one to four, and weigh approximately 1.5 kg. Cubs remain with the mother for about two years.

Reserves: Hluhluwe-iMfolozi; Kruger; Kgalagadi; Etosha; Moremi; Chobe; Hwange; Mana Pools; Kafue; South Luangwa; Upemba; Ruaha; Tsavo; Arusha; Lake Manyara; Ngorongoro; Serengeti; Virunga; Garamba; Kidepo; Murchison Falls; Queen Elizabeth; Marsabit; Samburu; Meru; Masai Mara; Nairobi; Amboseli; Tarangire; Selous; Mukumi.

GOLDEN CAT *Caracal (Profelis) aurata* SH 38–50 cm

Laila Bahaa-el-din

A robust, *medium-sized cat* (up to 16 kg), the males being larger in size than the females. The *tail is proportionally longer than in either the Serval or Caracal* and the *ears are smaller and rounded.* Pelage colour is very variable but is usually red-brown, although dark brown and grey animals are common in some areas. *Dark spots* are present to a greater or lesser extent *on the underparts* and in some animals over the entire body. This is a species of tropical forest and in some parts high montane areas. Because of the nature of its habitat it is rarely seen, even where densities are high. Rodents, hyrax and duikers form an important part of the diet, and it will also eat birds. Virtually nothing is known about its behaviour in the wild.

Reserves: Salonga; Ruwenzori; Virunga; Garamba; Queen Elizabeth.

LEOPARD *Panthera pardus* SH 70–80 cm

This elegant, powerfully built cat has black spots on the legs, flanks, hindquarters and head, *the spots on the rest of the body forming irregular circles or rosettes*. The general body colour ranges from grey-white to orange-russet, with white to off-white underparts. The tail is about half of the total length and has rosettes on the upper surface and a white tip. These cats are very variable in size, with those from southern areas averaging only 20 to 30 kg, compared to the north where animals of over 60 kg are not uncommon. Males are considerably larger than the females. The Leopard is found in all the major habitats, although it has been eradicated in many parts of South Africa. Pairs come together to mate but animals are otherwise solitary. It is active both at night and during the day but lies up during the hotter hours. Males defend a territory, marking it with urine, droppings, by scratching trees and by vocalization. A territory may encompass the home ranges of one or more females, the home-range size being dependent on the abundance of prey species; it may be as small as 10 km² or as large as several hundred square kilometres. Leopard have the most varied diet of any cats in the area, and will eat anything from insects, reptiles, birds and rodents up to large antelope. Larger kills are usually dragged to cover, or carried into trees if Lion or hyaenas are present. Two to three cubs, with a mass of some 500 g, may be born at any time of the year.

Reserves: Hluhluwe-iMfolozi; uMkhuzi; Kruger; Kgalagadi; Etosha; Moremi; Chobe; Hwange; Mana Pools; Kafue; South Luangwa; Upemba; Tsavo; Arusha; Lake Manyara; Ngorongoro; Serengeti; Virunga; Garamba; Murchison Falls; Queen Elizabeth; Mt Elgon; Marsabit; Samburu; Meru; Mt Kenya; Aberdares; Masai Mara; Nairobi; Amboseli.

CHEETAH *Acinonyx jubatus* SH 80 cm

Alan Weaving

Cheetah marking territory

Although similar to the Leopard in general appearance, this cat is longer in the leg and has a lighter, *greyhound-like build*. It is also distinguished by its *spots which are solid* and do not form rosettes, and by the *black line, or 'tear-mark' extending from the inner corner of each eye to the corner of the mouth*. The long tail is black-ringed with a white tip. Normally associated with open savanna and light woodland, it occasionally occurs in somewhat denser woodland and more hilly terrain. Adult males are solitary or may come together in small bachelor parties, but they apparently do not establish territories, whereas females do defend territories from which they drive other female Cheetah. Males move freely over female territories, and there is an elaborate, drawn-out courtship period. This cat is famed for its high-speed (more than 70 km/h) sprints when hunting but these can only be sustained for a few hundred metres. Antelope with a mass of up to 60 kg form the bulk of its prey. Litters of two to five are dropped at any time of the year. The cubs have a mantle of long, greyish hair down the back.

Reserves: Hluhluwe-iMfolozi; Kruger; Kgalagadi; Etosha; Chobe; Hwange; Kafue; South Luangwa; Tsavo; Ngorongoro; Serengeti; Marsabit; Samburu; Meru; Masai Mara; Amboseli.

CARACAL *Caracal caracal* SH 45 cm

A powerfully built cat with *hindquarters slightly higher than the shoulders*, and a short, uniformly coloured tail. The general fur colour varies from pale reddish-fawn to brick-red but the underparts are paler with faint blotching. Black and white patches, notably around the eyes and mouth, mark the face. The long, *pointed ears with tufts of long, black hair at the tips* are diagnostic; the backs of the ears are black with a liberal sprinkling of white hairs. This cat is very versatile and occupies most habitats. Although mainly nocturnal, in undisturbed areas it may also be seen in the early morning and late afternoon hours. The Caracal is solitary and males are probably territorial. It is predominantly a hunter of small- to medium-sized mammals.

Reserves: Table Mountain; Karoo; Mountain Zebra; uKhahlamba; Willem Pretorius; Kruger; Kgalagadi; Namib-Naukluft Park; Etosha; Moremi; Chobe; Hwange; Mana Pools; Kafue; South Luangwa; Tsavo; Ngorongoro; Serengeti; Mt Kenya.

SMALL SPOTTED CAT *Felis nigripes* SH 25 cm

Alex Sliwa

This, one of the smallest cat species (about 2 kg), is endemic to southern Africa. Pelage colour varies from reddish-fawn to off-white, with a liberal scattering of *black or red-brown spots and bars*. The short tail is black-ringed and -tipped and the *backs of the ears lack the reddish hair* of the African Wild Cat. This species inhabits open, dry areas with sparse plant cover. This cat preys mainly on small rodents and birds. It breeds well in captivity, with one to three kittens making up a litter.

Reserves: Karoo; Camdeboo; Mountain Zebra; Mokala.

AFRICAN WILD CAT *Felis silvestris lybica* SH 35 cm

Alex Sliwa

Very similar in general appearance to the domestic cat but it is larger and has proportionately longer legs. Body coloration is variable, ranging from pale tawny in drier areas to grey in regions with a higher rainfall. The extent of dark markings on the body and legs varies greatly but the *short, reddish-brown hair at the back of each ear* is characteristic. The relatively long, well-haired *tail is dark-ringed with a black tip*. This cat occurs in most habitats, even close to settlements where it breeds with the domestic cat. They are solitary animals that are active at night and males defend territories. Although small rodents are an important part of their diet, they will take prey up to the size of hares and a springhare. Kittens are born during the warm, wet months.

Reserves: Virtually all.

SERVAL *Leptailurus serval* SH 60 cm

John Carlyon

This *long-legged, spotted cat* has a *short, banded tail with a black tip*. General body colour varies greatly but is usually yellowish-fawn. The underparts are paler but also spotted. The *large, rounded ears* have a black tip and a white patch on the back surface. It inhabits areas of tall grassland, reedbeds and rank vegetation fringing forest, usually in association with water. It may be active at night or during the day, depending on the level of disturbance. The Serval is usually solitary but pairs and family parties are not uncommon. Small mammals, principally rodents, make up the bulk of their diet. Litters of one to five kittens are born in summer.

Reserves: uKhahlamba; Hluhluwe-iMfolozi; Kruger; Etosha; Moremi; Chobe; Hwange; Mana Pools; Kafue; South Luangwa; Nyika Plateau; Upemba; Tsavo; Ngorongoro; Serengeti; Virunga; Garamba; Queen Elizabeth; Marsabit; Samburu; Masai Mara.

CIVET *Civettictis civetta* SH 40 cm

Although similar to the genets (p. 74), the Civet is much larger (9–15 kg), has a proportionally shorter tail and longer legs. When walking it *holds its back in a distinctly arched position* and its head close to the ground. The overall fur colour is grey to grey-brown with numerous black spots, blotches and bands covering the body. The *white, black and grey facial markings* are distinctive. A ridge of dark hair along the spine is raised when the animal feels threatened. The *tail is banded below but black above and at the tip*. The Civet prefers woodland associations near permanent water. It is mainly nocturnal and crepuscular and forages alone or in pairs. It has a fixed home range, which it marks with mounds of droppings and anal-gland secretions. A wide range of food items are taken, up to the size of hares. Litters of two to four are born during the warm, wet months.

Reserves: Kruger; Mapungubwe; Etosha; Moremi; Chobe; Hwange; Mana Pools; Kafue; South Luangwa; Upemba; Gombe Stream; Tsavo; Arusha; Lake Manyara; Serengeti; Virunga; Garamba; Queen Elizabeth; Masai Mara; Meru; Samburu; Lake Nakuru.

SOUTH AFRICAN LARGE-SPOTTED GENET
Genetta tigrina TL 1.0 m

COMMON LARGE-SPOTTED GENET *Genetta maculata* TL 1.0 m

The markings and colour of this genet are very variable in different parts of its range, with two species and several subspecies now recognized. It is similar to the other genets in overall appearance but its spots are larger than in the Small-spotted Genet and they are *rusty brown* in colour. There is *no prominent crest* down the back and the hair is softer and shorter. The *tail tip is usually dark* and the chin is white. Its distribution is largely limited to habitats with fairly dense vegetation and permanent water. It feeds on insects, millipedes, snails, mice, lizards, birds and occasionally wild berries. Although the Large-spotted Genet does most of its hunting on the ground, it is extremely agile and readily hunts in trees and bushes.

Reserves: South African Large-spotted Genet: Table Mountain; Bontebok; Addo Elephant; uKhahlamba; Hluhluwe-iMfolozi; uMkhuzi; **Common Large-spotted Genet**: Kruger; Moremi; Chobe; Hwange; Mana Pools; South Luangwa; Serengeti; Virunga; Garamba; Queen Elizabeth.

SMALL-SPOTTED GENET *Genetta genetta* TL 92 cm

John Carlyon

This is the most widely distributed of the six genet species occurring in the region. The genets have *long, sleek bodies and tails*, short legs, and relatively long, rounded ears. This species has a crest of *black-tipped hair running down the back* and this is raised when the animal is alarmed. General body colour is off-white to greyish and liberally covered with dark brown to black spots and bars. The tail is ringed with black and usually has a white tip. This genet tolerates a very wide range of habitats, including isolated rock outcrops in arid areas. It is nocturnal and solitary. The genets eat a wide range of invertebrates, small rodents, birds and reptiles. Normally from two to four young are born per litter.

Reserves: Table Mountain; Bontebok; Karoo; Mapungubwe; Mountain Zebra; Willem Pretorius; Kruger; Pilanesberg; Kgalagadi; Namib-Naukluft; Etosha; Moremi; Chobe; Hwange; Upemba; Tsavo; Serengeti; Samburu; Masai Mara; Nairobi.

SPOTTED HYAENA *Crocuta crocuta* SH 85 cm

Alan Weaving

With its *heavily built forequarters, sloping back, large head* with prominent rounded ears, and *brown spotting*, this hyaena should not be mistaken for any other species. Its nightly *whoops, screams and cackles* which indicate its presence are one of Africa's best-known sounds. The Spotted Hyaena occurs in many different habitats but avoids forest. Once considered to be a cowardly scavenger, research has shown that it is an efficient hunter. It lives in family groups, known as clans, which are led by a female. The size of a clan varies from three to 15 or more individuals, with each clan defending a territory against other hyaenas. The *chalk-white droppings* are a clear indication of the animals' presence. They will eat anything from insects to big game, including Zebra, Giraffe and Blue Wildebeest. Clans frequently drive Lion and other predators from their kills. A litter usually comprises one to two cubs, which may be dropped at any time of the year.

Reserves: Hluhluwe-iMfolozi; Kruger; Addo Elephant; Kgalagadi; Namib-Naukluft; Etosha; Moremi; Chobe; Hwange; Mana Pools; Kafue; South Luangwa; Nyika Plateau; Upemba; Tsavo; Lake Manyara; Ngorongoro; Serengeti; Virunga; Garamba; Mt Elgon; Marsabit; Samburu; Meru; Masai Mara; Amboseli; Tarangire; Selous.

BROWN HYAENA *Hyaena brunnea* SH 80 cm

ABPL / Joan Ryder

M G L Mills

The forequarters of this hyaena are also heavily developed with shoulders higher than the rump, but it is distinguished by its *long, dark brown, shaggy coat*, the *light-coloured mantle on the shoulders and back*, and the *long, erect and pointed ears*. The short tail is bushy and dark in colour. This is a species with a wide habitat tolerance but it has been eradicated from much of its former range. In recent years, this hyaena has been reintroduced to a number of national parks and reserves within its former range. Most of its activity takes place at night and animals are usually solitary, although several animals may share a territory, apparently forming a family unit consisting of four to six individuals. The Brown Hyaena is not as vocal as the Spotted Hyaena. It is mainly a scavenger but will also feed on invertebrates, small vertebrates and wild fruits. Receptive females mate with nomadic males and not with males from within the group. A litter usually consists of two to three cubs, which may be born at any time of the year.

Reserves: iSimangaliso, Kruger, Pilanesberg, Addo Elephant; Mokala, Namaqua; Kgalagadi; Namib-Naukluft; Cape Cross Seal; Etosha; Hwange.

STRIPED HYAENA *Hyaena hyaena* SH 72 cm

This hyaena looks *like a large Aardwolf,* and is smaller than the Spotted Hyaena which shares the same range. It weighs from 40–55 kg. The *buff to grey shaggy coat is covered by numerous transverse black stripes,* and a *well-developed erectile mane* extends from the base of the neck to the rump. There are numerous stripes on the legs too. The head is very large and the throat area is mainly black. The ears are long and pointed, and the *tail is long and bushy.* It occurs in arid areas and often in association with rocky outcrops which provide shelter. An almost entirely nocturnal animal, it takes to dense bush or rock crevices during the daylight hours. The Striped Hyaena is omnivorous, taking large numbers of insects and other invertebrates, small mammals, birds, carrion, and also certain fruits. It forages alone or in pairs, and home ranges are probably quite large. From two to four cubs are born, usually in a rocky den, and these begin to accompany the adults only at some six months of age. In many ways this species of hyaena is similar to the Brown Hyaena, which is restricted to southern Africa. This is the least studied of the three hyaena species, yet has the widest distributional range. It occurs widely in East Africa, into North Africa, extending eastwards through the Arabian Peninsula as far east as Pakistan and India.

Reserves: Serengeti; Marsabit; Samburu; Tsavo.

AARDWOLF *Proteles cristatus* SH 50 cm

The Aardwolf has a *typical hyaena-like appearance* though it is much smaller than the hyaena species. The general colour is pale buff with *several black vertical stripes on the body* and black bands on the upperparts of the legs. The muzzle and feet are black and the bushy tail is black towards the tip. The ears are large and pointed. This harmless carnivore occupies a wide range of habitats and is found in both high- and low-rainfall areas but avoids forest. Although usually active at night, it frequently moves around in the cooler daylight hours. It may be solitary or live in pairs or in small family parties, and a home range is occupied by two or more individuals. More than one female may drop her pups in the same burrow; pups are generally born during the summer months. The bulk of the Aardwolf's food consists of termites but it will occasionally eat other insects. There is no evidence to support the claim that it kills and eats sheep, and although the canine teeth are well developed, the cheek teeth are small and not suited to eating flesh. Although harmless to domestic livestock, many are killed during problem animal control programmes targeting Black-backed Jackal and Caracal.

Reserves. Table Mountain, Bontebok, Karoo, Mountain Zebra; Willem Pretorius; Hluhluwe-iMfolozi; Kruger; Pilanesberg; Kgalagadi; Etosha; Chobe; Hwange; Tsavo; Serengeti; Nairobi; Samburu.

WILD DOG *Lycaon pictus* SH 72 cm

This is the largest member of the dog family occurring in Africa and is easily identified by the body colouring, which is *irregularly blotched with black, white, brown and yellowish-brown*. No two dogs have identical patterning. The muzzle is black, and a black line extends from the muzzle to between the ears which are dark in colour, large and rounded. The Wild Dog is a pack-hunter of the open plains and savanna woodland. Packs usually number from 10 to 15 individuals and nearly all hunting takes place during the day. They do not establish territories but their home ranges are very large. Hunting is a team effort and once a prey animal has been singled out, the pack pursues it at speeds of up to 50 km/h until the prey weakens and can be overpowered. Pups and adults that remain at the den are fed by the hunters with regurgitated meat. Antelope form the bulk of their prey. The pups are born during the dry, winter months when hunting conditions are at their best; they accompany the adults when they are about three months old.

Reserves: Addo Elephant; Hluhluwe-iMfolozi; Kruger; Etosha; Moremi; Chobe; Hwange; Mana Pools; Kafue; South Luangwa; Arusha; Ngorongoro; Serengeti; Virunga; Garamba; Samburu; Masai Mara.

GOLDEN (COMMON) JACKAL *Canis aureus* SH 38–50 cm

This jackal has a very wide distribution as it also occurs in North Africa, southern Europe and eastwards to India and south-east Asia. Although the coat colour is variable, the Golden Jackal is *usually pale gold-brown with black and grey hair on the back*. The head, ears and sides are sometimes reddish and the underparts are paler to off-white. The *tip of the tail is black*. This species favours open country with scatterings of bush and trees, but is very adaptable. It forms permanent pair-bonds and holds territories that range from 0.5–2.5 km² in size. Larger groups may come together temporarily where there is an abundance of food. In protected areas it is active at night and during the day but where it is persecuted it is purely nocturnal. Co-operation in hunting by mated pairs greatly increases prey capture success. Golden Jackals are omnivorous, taking fruits, small mammals, including the young of antelope, birds, reptiles and invertebrates, as well as carrion. There are usually five to six pups per litter which in Serengeti are dropped in January/February to coincide with the birth of Thomson's Gazelle lambs – an important source of food in this area. The young of the previous year, known as 'helpers', may assist in bringing food to the new litters.

Reserves: Serengeti; Masai Mara; Ngorongoro; Samburu; Marsabit.

BLACK-BACKED JACKAL *Canis mesomelas* SH 38 cm

This medium-sized, dog-like carnivore has a *white-flecked, black 'saddle'* that is broadest at the neck and shoulders and narrows towards the base of the tail. The face, flanks and legs vary in colour from grey-brown to reddish-brown, and there is white on the lips, throat and chest. The *bushy tail is mainly black*. Most habitats are utilized by this jackal, with the exception of forest. In areas where they ·are not disturbed they are most frequently active during the cooler daylight hours but in many areas they are nocturnal. Normally they forage alone or in pairs, but in some areas they may come together temporarily in groups of six or more. Pairs form a long-term pair-bond and both members mark and defend a territory against other jackals. They have a *characteristic screaming yell which ends with three or four yaps*, and this is most frequently heard during the mating season, which in the south is in the winter months. The Black-backed Jackal will eat virtually any food, including carrion, small antelope, mice, reptiles, insects and wild fruits. From one to six pups are born between July and October in the southern part of their range.

Reserves: Karoo; Addo Elephant; Namaqua; Camdeboo; Mountain Zebra; Mokala; uKhahlamba; Willem Pretorius; Hluhluwe-iMfolozi; uMkhuzi; Kruger; Kgalagadi; Namib-Naukluft; Etosha; Hwange; Ngorongoro; Serengeti; Marsabit; Samburu; Masai Mara; Nairobi.

SIDE-STRIPED JACKAL *Canis adustus* SH 40 cm

John Carlyon

John Carlyon

Although similar in general appearance to the Black-backed Jackal, this species has a distinctive coat colour. From a distance it has an *overall grey appearance* but closer up a *lighter coloured band fringed with black* is noticeable *along each flank*, hence its common name. The underparts are slightly paler but the *bushy tail* is predominantly black with a *white tip*. It prefers well-watered areas in woodland and is commonly associated with human settlements, but despite this it is secretive and not often seen. It is also much quieter than the Black-backed Jackal and when it does call, it is usually in a series of yaps. Some African tribes are said to value the skins and claws of this species as a means of warding off evil spirits. A largely solitary animal, it is most active at night although may be seen in the early morning or late afternoon. Its food is varied – ranging from mammals, to birds, carrion and wild fruits – but not to the same extent as the Black-backed Jackal. In the southern part of its range pups are born between August and January. There are usually between four and six pups per litter, which are born in the abandoned burrows of other species.

Reserves: iSimangaliso; Kruger; Moremi; Chobe; Hwange; Mana Pools; Kafue; South Luangwa; Kundelungu; Upemba; Ngorongoro; Serengeti; Virunga; Queen Elizabeth; Masai Mara; Nairobi; Selous; Ruaha.

BAT-EARED FOX *Otocyon megalotis* SH 35 cm

Nigel Dennis / IOA

A small (up to 5 kg), jackal-like carnivore with *very large distinctive ears* (14 cm long). The body is covered in quite long, silvery-grey hair with a distinctly grizzled appearance. The legs are black, as is the upper surface of the bushy tail. *When running it arches its back slightly.* This fox occurs in most habitats but avoids high mountains, dense woodland and forest. Both nocturnal and diurnal activity is common but it is least active during the warmer midday hours. Groups usually number from two to six individuals and, because pairs mate for life, these usually comprise a pair and its offspring. Larger groupings are temporary and are usually associated with an abundant, localized source of food. These animals dig their own burrows but also take over those dug by other species. Termites and other insects make up the bulk of the diet but reptiles, rodents and fruits are also eaten. Litters consist of four to six pups.

Reserves: Karoo; Mokala; Mountain Zebra; Kruger; Kgalagadi; Namib-Naukluft; Etosha; Chobe; Hwange; Tsavo; Lake Manyara; Serengeti; Samburu; Masai Mara; Nairobi; Amboseli.

CAPE FOX *Vulpes chama* SH 30 cm

Alan Weaving

Adult female and pups

This is the only 'true' fox occurring within the area and is also the smallest (2.5–4.0 kg). The *back and sides are grizzled silvery-grey* in colour and the neck, chest and forelegs are pale tawny to almost white. The ears are long and pointed but not to the same extent as in the Bat-eared Fox. The principal identification character is the *long, bushy tail* which is generally darker in colour than the body fur. It has a wide habitat tolerance but shows a preference for grassland and arid scrub-covered plains. In the extreme southern part of its range it is associated with dense stands of lowland fynbos, or macchia, and extensive wheatlands. These animals are normally solitary and mostly active at night when they commonly give vent to a high-pitched howl and bark, particularly during the August to October breeding season. They are active diggers and will excavate their own burrows if nothing else is available. During the day they lie up in holes, dense scrub or in rock crevices. Each animal defends a small territory within a larger home range. A wide variety of food items is utilized but of these, insects are most important. Carrion, other invertebrates and reptiles are occasionally taken. In parts of their range they are blamed for killing and eating young lambs and as a result several thousand foxes are killed by farmers each year. Although there is some basis for these claims, they appear to be exaggerated. Pups are born in the spring and summer months after a gestation period of 52 days. Two females may drop their pups in the same burrow.

Reserves: Bontebok; Karoo; Mokala; Mountain Zebra; Addo Elephant; Willem Pretorius; Kgalagadi; Namib-Naukluft; Etosha.

CAPE CLAWLESS OTTER *Aonyx capensis* TL 1.3 m

A large otter (up to 18 kg) that could only be confused with the Congo Clawless Otter where their ranges overlap. It is heavily built with a long, somewhat flattened tail. The soft, short, dark brown *coat appears black when wet*; the lips, chin and throat are silvery-white. The toes are finger-like and lack claws although some digits of the hindfeet have small, flat, rudimentary nails. *On land it walks with its back distinctly arched*, and in water usually swims with only the head visible. For an otter it has an amazing habitat tolerance, penetrating arid areas along riverbeds with permanent pools and also utilizing coastal waters. It may be active at any time but lies up under cover during the hotter daylight hours. These animals may be solitary or occur in pairs and family parties. Although they can hunt by sight in the water, much of their food is extricated from under rocks or in mud by means of the 'fingers'. Crabs form the bulk of their diet but they also feed on fish, amphibians, small mammals and birds. Otter cubs are usually born in a holt (shallow burrow) or amongst rocks and vegetation where they are hidden.

Reserves: Table Mountain; De Hoop; Garden Route; Richtersveld; Karoo; uKhahlamba; iSimangaliso; uMkhuzi; Hluhluwe-iMfolozi; Kruger; Moremi; Chobe; Kafue; Ngorongoro; Serengeti; Virunga; Garamba; Masai Mara.

SPOTTED-NECKED OTTER *Hydrictis maculicollis* TL 1.0 m

This is the smallest of the three otter species in the area, rarely with mass of over 5 kg. It has short, uniformly dark brown to reddish-brown fur with *paler blotching on the throat and upper chest*. The feet are webbed and each toe has a claw. This otter is closely associated with permanent, clear water and *never occurs at the coast* or far from water. Groups of two to six – occasionally more – are active during the day and maintain contact by whistling. Fish are important in the diet but this otter will also eat crabs, frogs, birds and insects. Prey is normally taken to the banks to be eaten although may be consumed in the water. Like the Cape Clawless Otter, this species uses 'latrine' sites which it establishes close to the water's edge. Litters of two to three cubs are probably born during the summer after a gestation period of 60 days.

Reserves: uKhahlamba; Kruger; Moremi; Chobe; Kafue; Gombe Stream; Rubando Island; Salonga; Maiko; Virunga; Garamba.

HONEY BADGER *Mellivora capensis* SH 30 cm

An unmistakable carnivore that is *powerfully built with short legs and very small eyes*. The body hair is short with the *top of the head, neck and back being silvery-grey* in colour and the *underparts and legs black*. The short tail is usually held erect when the animal is walking. It occurs in all the major habitats. In most areas it is nocturnal, but in places where it has not been disturbed it will forage during the cooler daylight hours. Solitary animals and pairs are usually encountered. Rodents and invertebrates make up the bulk of their diet but they also feed on carrion, reptiles and birds. As the common name suggests they are also partial to raiding beehives. From one to four young (usually one or two) may be born at any time of the year.

Reserves: Karoo; Agulhas; Garden Route; Hluhluwe-iMfolozi; Kruger; Kgalagadi; Etosha; Chobe; Hwange; Mana Pools; Kafue; South Luangwa; Upemba; Tsavo; Ngorongoro; Serengeti; Maiko; Virunga; Queen Elizabeth; Masai Mara; Meru; Samburu; Selous; Ruaha.

STRIPED (WHITE-NAPED) WEASEL
Poecilogale albinucha TL 45 cm

A long, slender member of the mustelid family with *very short legs*, enabling it to enter rodent burrows. The overall body colour is black with *four off-white to yellowish stripes* extending from the neck to the tail base. The *top of the head is white*. Although it is frequently confused with the Striped Polecat its body hair is much shorter and it has no white facial patches. It shows a marked preference for open grassland. This species is mainly nocturnal and may be encountered on its own, in pairs or in family parties. It is a very efficient digger but frequently shelters in rodent burrows too. Small rodents are its principal prey. The young weigh only 4 g at birth (adult 300 g), and are born mainly in the summer months.

Reserves: Willem Pretorius; Hluhluwe-iMfolozi; Kgalagadi; Upemba; Virunga; Queen Elizabeth.

STRIPED POLECAT (ZORILLA) *Ictonyx striatus* TL 62 cm

This is a small (up to 1.4 kg), distinctly marked carnivore with long, shiny black body hair broken by *four distinct white stripes* extending from the top of the head to the base of the tail and by *white facial patches*. The *tail is predominantly white* but has black flecking. A species that occurs in all the major habitats, it is strictly nocturnal and a solitary forager. Although it can dig its own burrows, it normally makes use of other animals' shelters. Insects and small rodents form the bulk of its prey. Large numbers of this species are killed on roads. One to three young are born during summer.

Reserves: Virtually all.

SMALL GREY MONGOOSE *Galerella pulverulenta* TL 62 cm

 Although similar in appearance to the Large Grey Mongoose, this carnivore is much smaller (up to 1.0 kg) and *lacks the black tail tip*. Body and tail colour is uniform light to dark grey *with distinct grizzling*. The legs are usually dark brown to black. It occurs in most habitats, ranging from coastal forest to high mountains and is almost exclusively active during daylight. It is a predominantly solitary animal. This mongoose makes use of well-used pathways within its home range and is probably at least partly territorial. Small rodents and invertebrates form the bulk of its food. From one to three helpless young are born from about August to December.

Reserves: Table Mountain; Bontebok; Karoo; Mountain Zebra; Addo Elephant; Namaqua; West Coast; Garden Route.

LARGE GREY (EGYPTIAN) MONGOOSE
Herpestes ichneumon TL 1.0 m

This large mongoose (up to 4 kg) has *long, grey-grizzled body hair* but the lower legs and feet are black. The *tail* is distinctly *black-tipped*. It favours densely vegetated and well-watered areas, and is predominantly diurnal. Solitary animals or pairs are usually observed. These animals frequently stand up on their hindlegs to check their surroundings. Small rodents form the principal food but they also take a wide range of other small vertebrates and invertebrates. A litter size of two to four is usual, most of which are born during the summer months.

Reserves: Agulhas; Garden Route; iSimangaliso; Kruger; Moremi; Chobe; Mana Pools; Kafue; South Luangwa; Kundelungu; Virunga; Garamba; Queen Elizabeth; Marsabit; Masai Mara; Samburu.

SLENDER MONGOOSE *Galerella sanguinea* TL 58 cm

A slender, short-legged mongoose that varies in overall body colour from grizzled yellow-brown or grey to chestnut-orange. However, all colour forms have a *distinctive black tip to the tail*. When the animal runs the tail is held well clear of the ground, often curving forward over the back. It occurs in many different habitats, the principle requirement being adequate cover. Single animals are commonly seen, and although they are mainly terrestrial, they climb readily. Small vertebrates and invertebrates are eaten. Litters consist of only one or two young and births coincide with the warm, wet months.

Reserves: Hluhluwe-iMfolozi; uMkhuzi; Kruger; Pilanesberg; Kgalagadi; Etosha; Moremi; Chobe; Hwange; Mana Pools; Kafue; South Luangwa; Tsavo; Serengeti; Virunga; Garamba; Marsabit; Masai Mara; Nairobi; Lake Bogoria; Meru.

WATER MONGOOSE *Atilax paludinosus* TL 80 cm–1 m

A large (up to 5.5 kg) *shaggy-haired* mongoose, usually dark brown but some are reddish-brown or almost black. The *hair often has a glossy sheen* and there are no distinctive markings. As its name suggests this mongoose is associated with well-watered areas, such as rivers, dams, estuaries, swamps and marine margins. It may penetrate arid areas by following dry stream-beds with a scattering of permanent pools. Although it is mainly active at night, it is also crepuscular. Home ranges tend to be linear, in that the animal follows the banks and shorelines of water-bodies. It follows regular pathways when foraging and swims readily. Crabs and amphibians make up the bulk of its diet but it will also eat birds, rodents, insects and reptiles. In the south one to three kittens are born between August and December.

Reserves: Table Mountain; Bontebok; Karoo; Mountain Zebra; uKhahlamba; Hluhluwe-iMfolozi; uMkhuzi; Kruger; Moremi; Kafue; South Luangwa; Kasanka; Blue Lagoon; Lochinvar; Upemba; Virunga; Garamba; Queen Elizabeth; Masai Mara; Nairobi.

DWARF MONGOOSE *Helogale parvula* TL 38 cm

This is the *smallest mongoose* in the area, with an average mass of 300 g. It is uniformly dark brown in colour and looks almost black from a distance. The fur is slightly grizzled and distinctly glossy. A species of the open woodland and grassland savanna, it is commonly associated with rocky areas. Dwarf Mongoose troops, usually numbering about 10 individuals, live in a fixed home range and the dens are usually located in termite mounds. A rigid social system, with a dominant male and female at the head of each troop, places each individual in a distinct 'pecking order'. Only the dominant female breeds but, apart from suckling, she leaves the care of the young to the other troop members. Insects make up the bulk of the diet.

Reserves: Kruger; Etosha; Moremi; Chobe; Hwange; Mana Pools; Kafue; South Luangwa; Tsavo; Ngorongoro; Serengeti; Mikumi; Ruaha; Masai Mara; Nairobi; Samburu.

WHITE-TAILED MONGOOSE *Ichneumia albicauda* TL 1.2 m

John Carlyon

This is a *very large* mongoose (up to 5.2 kg) and when walking holds its *rump slightly higher than its shoulders*. The coarse, shaggy hair is brown-grey to almost black on the body and long legs, and the well-haired *white tail* is distinctive. This mongoose frequents woodland savanna and, to a lesser extent, forest. It is poorly known as a result of its exclusive nocturnal activity. It is a solitary forager, taking a wide range of prey items up to the size of cane-rats. Young are probably dropped in spring and early summer.

Reserves: Hluhluwe-iMfolozi; uMkhuzi; Kruger; Chobe; Hwange; Mana Pools; Kafue; South Luangwa; Kasanka; Blue Lagoon; Lochinvar; Upemba; Tsavo; Serengeti; Virunga; Queen Elizabeth; Hell's Gate; Masai Mara; Amboseli; Lake Bogoria; Lake Nakuru; Meru.

BANDED MONGOOSE *Mungos mungo* TL 55 cm

A small (up to 1.6 kg) grizzled-grey to grey-brown mongoose with *10 to 12 dark-brown to black transverse bands* extending from behind the shoulders to the base of the tail. The *tail is bushy*, unlike the thinly haired tail of the Suricate. A distinct preference is shown for woodland where there is adequate ground-cover. Troops of five to 30 individuals live together in a relatively small home range (up to 4 km²) and will make use of several shelters scattered through the area. Contact between different troops may result in clashes but apparently these animals are not territorial. Their diet consists of a wide range of invertebrates, as well as reptiles, birds and mice. The two to six youngsters in a litter suckle from any lactating female in the troop.

Reserves: Hluhluwe-iMfolozi; uMkhuzi; Kruger; Etosha; Moremi; Chobe; Hwange; Kafue; South Luangwa; Upemba; Serengeti; Ruwenzori; Virunga; Garamba; Queen Elizabeth; Amboseli; Meru; Samburu.

YELLOW MONGOOSE *Cynictis penicillata* TL 50 cm

A small mongoose (less than 1 kg) with two principal colour forms occurring: *reddish-yellow with a white-tipped tail*, and greyish without a white tail tip. The latter form is mainly restricted to Botswana. Paler areas of hair are located on the chin, throat and upper chest. It is absent from areas with dense vegetation, and occurs mainly in open, short grassland and semi-desert scrub. A diurnal mongoose, it usually forages alone but lives in small colonies of five to 10. They usually dig their own burrows but will also share those of the Suricate and Ground Squirrel. Most of their food consists of insects and other invertebrates. Litters of two to five are born in summer.

Reserves: Karoo; Mountain Zebra; Camdeboo; Namaqua; De Hoop; Kgalagadi; Chobe; Nxai Pan; Etosha; Namib-Naukluft.

SURICATE *Suricata suricatta* TL 50 cm

The body colour of this species varies from fawn to silvery-grey with *a number of darker, irregular, transverse bars* extending from just behind the shoulders to the base of the tail. The thin, tapering tail is short-haired and dark-tipped and *is held erect* when the animal runs. These animals frequently sit on their haunches using the tail as a support. They occur only in open, lightly vegetated areas with low rainfall. Suricates live in troops of up to 40 individuals and are active diggers. They are active during the day only, and insects and other invertebrates make up the bulk of their food.

Reserves: Karoo; Mountain Zebra; Willem Pretorius; Kgalagadi; Camdeboo; Namaqua; Namib-Naukluft; Skeleton Coast.

CAPE FUR SEAL *Arctocephalus pusillus* TL 1.6–2.2 m

Pup suckling

This is the only resident seal occurring in the area, with more than one million animals located in 23 breeding colonies on off-shore islands and on the mainland. The large size, *limbs modified to form flippers*, the presence of *small ears* and the animals' *location on the coast* make this an easy species to identify. When they move on land they bring the hindlimbs forward and bend the foreflippers outwards. Females are usually brownish-grey and males tend to be darker, but both appear much darker when wet; newborn pups have a black coat. Males may have a mass of as much as 300 kg during the summer, and in mid-October mature bulls move to the breeding colonies where they establish and defend territories. Cows arrive in November to give birth and then mate with the territorial bulls five to six days later. Territories and harems break up before the end of December. All feeding is done at sea, food comprising mainly shoaling fish such as pilchards but also squid and crustaceans.

Reserves: Cape Cross Seal; Agulhas; Namaqua; West Coast.

DUGONG *Dugong dugong* TL 2.5–3 m

P K Anderson

This entirely aquatic animal has a characteristic *cigar-shaped body* and forelimbs modified into paddle-like flippers but has *no hindlimbs*. It is greyish-brown in colour though slightly darker above than below and the skin has a scattering of bristles. The Dugong *inhabits the shallow, protected waters of bays and lagoons* but moves between these areas along shallow coastlines. It has a wide distribution in suitable habitat in the warmer parts of the Indian Ocean, from the Red Sea southwards to Mozambique, although stragglers are occasionally seen in northern KwaZulu-Natal. In East Africa the best chance of observing these animals is between Lamu and Malindi, Rufiji to Mafia and around the coastline of Pemba and Zanzibar islands. Dugong numbers have been greatly reduced in recent years as a result of hunting, pollution and siltation of the animal's feeding areas. In the past, sightings of herds of 500 animals were not unusual but today such numbers are rare and most herds consist of a family group, or several such groupings coming together at feeding sites: six to 30 animals is usual. They feed on sea-grasses and other aquatic vegetation and an adult can consume 30 kg each day. A single young is born and breeding seems to take place in July and August, although in Mozambique a November to January peak has been recorded.

Reserves: None.

Note: *The closely related West African Manatee (Trichechus senegalensis) occurs from Senegal to Angola and, although occasionally recorded on the coastline, it lives mainly in the major river systems. As it penetrates the Congo River it occurs within the area covered by this book.*

PRIMATES Order Primates

Africa has a rich primate fauna, which includes the Western and Eastern Gorilla, Common Chimpanzee, Bonobo, many typical 'long-tailed' monkeys, baboons and bushbabies. Many of these occur within the area covered by this book, with the lowest diversity occurring in the south.

The majority of species are associated with forest habitats but some occur in more open woodland. The most widespread primate in the area is, of course, man (*Homo sapiens*).

EASTERN GORILLA *Gorilla beringei* ♂1.7 m, ♀1.5 m

WESTERN GORILLA *Gorilla gorilla* ♂1.7 m, ♀1.5 m

Western Lowland Gorilla

This is the *largest of all primates* with males in the wild weighing up to 180 kg. Two gorilla species are recognized, the Western and Eastern, each of which has two subspecies. In the west, these are the Western Lowland and the Cross River, in the east the Eastern Lowland and the Mountain Gorilla. Probably more than 100 000 Gorillas survive in the wild, of which only some 700 are of the Mountain form. The main threats to gorilla survival include direct hunting for their meat and supposed medicinal value of body parts, as well as habitat loss. The general appearance of all subspecies is similar, with slight differences evident in coloration, hair length and skull structure. The *coat is black to greyish-black*, becoming greyer as the animal ages, and *adult males*

Mountain Gorilla

Roland Wirth

have a broad, whitish-silver 'saddle' on the back. Despite their fearsome appearance and large size, Gorillas are harmless, peaceful animals. They live in small groups ranging from two to 35 members, although between five and 10 is most usual. These groups are fairly stable and group members may remain together for long periods. Their home ranges are small (5–30 km²) and because their main food of leaves is abundant, only a tiny portion of this range is covered each day. At night they make nests of branches and leaves, either on the ground or up in trees. Groups are not territorial and home ranges overlap considerably. Each group is led and controlled by a silverback male, the remaining members comprising females and their young of different ages. On reaching maturity, females move to join another group and males leave the group to start their own harems. There may be considerable aggression between adult males competing for females. Gorillas do not have any particular breeding season and will produce a single young of 2 kg at any time of the year after a gestation period of about 260 days. Breeding begins at about 10 years of age.

Reserves: Kahuzi-Biega; Maiko; Virunga; Bwindi.

COMMON CHIMPANZEE *Pan troglodytes*
TL 70–92 cm, Upright ♂ >1 m

The *human-like appearance* of this species makes it unmistakable. Its coat is somewhat sparse and animals frequently go bald but where there is *fur it is black*. Skin on the hands and feet is black but *facial skin varies from pink to black*, with older animals usually having darker faces than younger ones. Animals in the wild weigh considerably less than captives, the males being heavier (40 kg) than the females (30 kg). The Common Chimpanzee is very vocal, with the most far-carrying call being the 'pant-hoot'. It has a much wider habitat tolerance than the Gorilla, occurring in various forest types, mixed woodland savanna and even in the open grasslands adjacent to these. These primates live in communities of 50 to 120 individuals which occupy ranges of up to 50 km². They forage alone in favoured core areas, or in parties of three to six animals. In some regions communities are migratory, moving over areas that may exceed 400 km². Males seldom leave the community into which they are born but females, when sexually mature, move to join neighbouring communities. A single young is born at any time of the year after a gestation period of about 240 days. These animals feed on a wide variety of foods, particularly fruits, but will also eat insects and meat if it is available. This is one of the few animals, other than man, that has mastered the art of using tools. These are used variously to 'fish' for termites, as clubs, and to crack nuts. All three subspecies that are recognized have declined in number as a result of habitat loss, hunting and the capture of young animals for the zoo and pet trade. The Common Chimpanzee does not occur south of the Congo River, where it is replaced by the Bonobo.

Reserves: Gombe Stream; Mahale Mountains; Kahuzi-Biega; Maiko; Virunga; Garamba; Murchison Falls; Queen Elizabeth.

BONOBO *Pan paniscus* Upright ♂ >1 m

Despite its other common name of Pygmy Chimpanzee, the Bonobo is similar in size to its cousin, the Common Chimpanzee, although the *body frame is lighter and the limbs are longer.* This more slender build has led some to refer to this species as the Gracile Chimpanzee. The *coat is black and the face is always black.* A *white 'tail-tuft'* is usually present. It is restricted to humid forest south of the Congo River and so its range does not overlap with the previous species at all. Bonobos also live in communities ranging from six to 15 individuals, and these tend to be more stable than in the Common Chimpanzee. Sex ratios within the groups are equal. Fruit makes up the bulk of the diet. Unlike the Common Chimpanzee, which often resorts to violence to solve conflict with troop members, the Bonobo is comparatively placid and resolves potential conflict situations by engaging in sex. This activity may be heterosexual as well as homosexual, also between young and adults. During the morning and late afternoon they usually feed high up in the trees where they can move rapidly if alarmed. During the hotter midday hours most foraging is done on the forest floor. At night they sleep in self-constructed branch and leaf nests more than 20 m above the ground. Little research has been carried out on this interesting species and few are kept in captivity. A single young, weighing about 1.5 kg, may be born at any time of the year.

Reserves: Salonga.

OLIVE BABOON *Papio (cynocephalus) anubis* TL up to 1.8 m

There is some controversy as to whether this baboon and the Chacma Baboon should be treated as a single or separate species. Recent thinking follows the belief that they are one and the same species and should be called either the Savanna or Common Baboon. Whatever is finally decided, these baboons have much in common and differences, where these occur, are small. The general build of the Olive and Chacma Baboon is the same, both showing a *back that slopes gently from the shoulders to the rump, long, slender arms,* and a *large, 'dog-like' head.* General behaviour is also very similar to that of the Chacma Baboon. The overall body colour is olive-brown, and there is a well defined cape of long hair. The so-called Yellow Baboon of Central and East Africa lacks a cape and is yellowish-brown in colour with paler underparts. The *tail has a typically 'broken' or kinked appearance.* These baboons feed mainly on a variety of plants, but will also kill and eat small mammals, such as young antelope and hares. They also come into conflict with man when they raid crops and in some areas they are heavily persecuted because of this. Female baboons of both species develop large, perineal swellings, dark pink in colour, which indicates to the adult males when they are ready for mating. The gestation period is six months and a single young is born. The young infant clings to its mother's chest for the first few weeks, but as it grows older it rides on her back. The Olive Baboon is one of the most frequently observed primates in East Africa.

Reserves: Kundelungu; Salonga; Gombe Stream; Arusha; Lake Manyara; Ngorongoro; Serengeti; Murchison Falls; Mt Elgon; Mt Kenya; Nairobi; Samburu; Meru; Lake Nakuru; Amboseli; Tsavo.

CHACMA BABOON *Papio (cynocephalus) ursinus* TL 1.0–1.6 m

Some authorities now recognize this baboon as a full species, *Papio ursinus*. This is a slender and relatively lightly built primate, although the males have powerfully built shoulders and head and weigh up to 45 kg. The head is somewhat dog-like and the posture of the long tail, which has a 'broken' appearance, is characteristic. The body has a covering of coarse hair which may be light grey to dark grey-brown. The hair on the upper-surface of the hands and feet is dark brown to black. Chacma Baboons are very widely distributed, occurring in most areas where there are rocky cliffs or tall trees for sleeping at night and permanent water. In some areas this baboon is heavily persecuted as it does on occasion raid crops and will kill sheep and goats. This is a very social species with troops averaging 15 individuals but numbers up to 100 are not uncommon in some areas. Troops consist of a dominant adult male and his 'lieutenants': low-ranking males, adult females and youngsters of all ages. The dominant male determines the troop's movements and he mates with the oestrus females. The bark, or 'bogom', of the Chacma Baboon is a typical sound of the African bush. These baboons are omnivorous and there is in fact little that they do not eat. A single young is born at any time of the year.

Reserves: Table Mountain; Mountain Zebra; uKʼhahlamba; Hluhluwe-iMfolozi; uMkhuzi; Kruger; Moremi; Chobe; Hwange; Mana Pools; South Luangwa.

VERVET (GREEN) MONKEY
Cercopithecus pygerythrus TL 95 cm–1.3 m

This is a very well known monkey and is often found close to human habitation. Six species of 'vervet' monkey are now recognized but all are very similar and should not be confused with other species outside this group. It is one of the most widespread and common of the diurnal primates. The hair is coarse, fairly long and *overall grizzled-grey* in colour, although the *face is black with a rim of pale to white hair*. The short hair on the upper surfaces of the hands and feet is black. The adult male has a distinctive *powder-blue scrotum*. It is a common species in woodland savanna and riverine woodland. Troops of 20 or more may be formed but smaller groups are more usual. Each troop has a very strict social ranking. Vervet Monkeys are exclusively diurnal and sleep in trees at night. They take a wide range of plant foods, insects and occasionally small vertebrates. A single young may be born at any time of the year.

Reserves: Addo Elephant; Hluhluwe-iMfolozi; uMkhuzi; Kruger; Karoo; Moremi; Chobe; Hwange; Mana Pools; Kafue; South Luangwa; Serengeti; Selous; Tsavo; Lake Naivasha; Nairobi; Amboseli; Lake Nakuru; Masai Mara; Meru; Samburu.

SYKES'S (BLUE) MONKEY *Cercopithecus albogularis* TL 1.2–1.4 m

This is a larger and much darker monkey than the Vervet, and a number of distinctly marked subspecies are recognized. Recent thinking has raised several of these subspecies to full species status. The southern form has a grizzled grey-brown back and sides but the hair on the legs and shoulders is dark brown or black. *Extent of white is variable on throat and underparts.* The *long hair on the forehead and cheeks* is distinctive, and the long tail is black for the last two-thirds of its length. This monkey is restricted to indigenous forest, although it will forage along the margins. Troops may number as many as 30 but most groups are smaller and spend most of their time in trees, rarely coming to the ground. They have a very distinctive bark ('jack') which carries far through the forest. Their principal foods include fruits, flowers, gum, leaves and seeds. Young are born in the summer months. In southern Africa it is often called Samango Monkey.

Reserves: iSimangaliso; Hluhluwe-iMfolozi; Ndumo; Kruger; Nyika Plateau; Mt Kilimanjaro; Salonga; Virunga; Mt Kenya; Lake Nakuru; Aberdares; Meru; Shimba Hills.

OWL-FACED MONKEY *Cercopithecus hamlyni* TL 1.1 m

A medium-sized monkey with a large, rounded face characterized by a *conspicuous narrow, vertical band that runs from the forehead to the upper lip.* The upperparts are dark olive-green and the underparts and legs are black. The tail is relatively short and thick and tipped by a black, bushy tassel. This monkey is restricted to dense rain and montane forest, and lives in small troops that are led by a single adult male. It feeds on fruit, leaves and insects. Little is known about its behaviour but, although it is rumoured to be partly night active, this remains to be confirmed.

Reserves: Kahuzi-Biega; Virunga.

Note: *The* Cercopithecus *monkeys form a very large and complex group, with at least 17 species occurring in Africa, of which 12 are found in the area covered by this book. Many are poorly known and have not been studied in the wild. The following species may be observed in the natural forests of Central and East Africa: Redtail Monkey (Cercopithecus ascanius) – NE and E Democratic Republic of Congo, S Uganda, W Kenya, W Tanzania and Rwanda; Moustached Monkey (C. cephus) – extreme north-west of the region; L'Hoest's Monkey (C. l'hoesti) – E Democratic Republic of Congo, W Uganda and Rwanda; Spot-nosed Monkey (C. nictitans) – NW Democratic Republic of Congo; Crowned Guenon (C. pogonias) – NW Democratic Republic of Congo; De Brazza's Monkey (C. neglectus) – Democratic Republic of Congo, W Kenya and Uganda; Wolf's Monkey (C. wolfi) – Democratic Republic of Congo and W Uganda; Dryas Monkey (C. dryas) – Democratic Republic of Congo.*

MONA MONKEY *Cercopithecus mona* TL 1.2 m

This is a medium-sized (up to 6 kg) monkey that has a *slate-blue face* with a contrasting *flesh-coloured muzzle*. A greyish-white band on its forehead separates the face from the dark crown, and there is a *black stripe running from the eye to the ear*. The crown and shoulders are olive-green, the rump is somewhat darker and the underparts are white. The outer surface of the forelimbs is black and the tail is dark above and white or yellow below. This species inhabits rain forests, where it feeds on fruit, shoots and insects. It lives in fairly large troops which may contain one or more adult males. The common name 'Mona' is derived from the contact call uttered by the female. A number of races and subspecies of the Mona Monkey are recognized, of which most occur in the western parts of their range. In several cases some authorities are of the opinion that the variations are great enough to warrant full species status.

Reserves: Virunga.

GUEREZA BLACK AND WHITE COLOBUS
Colobus guereza TL 95 cm–1.5 m

Pat Frere

This colobus monkey, also known as the Guereza, is very distinctive, with a 'V'-shaped mantle of white hair extending down the sides and along the lower back, and contrasting with the shorter black body hair. The long, predominantly black tail is bushy with a white area towards the tip, and the face is encircled by a 'beard' of short white hair. Albinos are commonly sighted on Mt Kenya. There is considerable variety and several distinct subspecies are recognized. These animals have a fairly wide habitat tolerance, ranging from bamboo thickets and various forest associations to wooded savanna, the only requirement being that adequate water and green-leaf food is available. They are highly arboreal but will descend to the ground on occasion. These monkeys have been recorded as wading waist-deep in water to eat aquatic

plants, but feed mainly on selected tree leaves. Troops of up to 50 individuals have been recorded but smaller numbers are more usual. Home ranges are small and probably bear relation to the abundance of suitable food. Small splinter groups move in loose association, and it is rare, particularly with large troops, for all the troop members to congregate together at one time. Young may be dropped at any time of the year and are almost pure white at birth.

Reserves: Mt Kilimanjaro; Virunga; Garamba; Queen Elizabeth; Mau Forest; Lake Naivasha; Lake Nakuru; Aberdares; Mt Kenya.

Note: *Three other species of 'Black' colobus which occur in West, Central and East Africa are: the Satanic Colobus (Colobus satanas); the Western Black and White Colobus (C. polykomos); and the Angola Black and White Colobus (C. angolensis). Only the Angola Black and White Colobus occurs in part of the area occupied by the Guereza Black and White Colobus, or Guereza, and can be distinguished as it lacks the white mantle around the back, but does have long, white hair patches on the shoulders and the white facial whiskers are well developed. The tail is not as bushy as that of the Guereza.*

PATAS MONKEY *Erythrocebus patas* TL ♂ up to 1.6 m

This is the *'greyhound'* of the monkey-world, well-adapted with its *long legs and slender body* to a mainly terrestrial existence. The *coat is short and coarse. Males are brick-red* in colour, up to 10 kg and have a *bright blue scrotum; females and young have more yellowish coats*. The underparts are pale to white. *Facial markings are distinctive*, comprising a *white moustache* which contrasts with the dark face, and a *white patch on the nose*. Unlike other monkeys the Patas *avoids dense cover and occupies dry savanna* and rocky habitats, although it does climb into trees to sleep at night. Troops in East Africa may number up to 50 individuals but smaller troops are more common. Each troop has a dominant female and one adult male, and a distinct 'pecking order' is maintained. The male spends much of his time on the alert, watching for potential danger, and is often seen standing on its hindlegs for a better view. Unlike forest monkeys, Patas troops may cover large areas. They feed on a wide range of plants as well as on some insects. The young are dropped between January and May.

Reserves: Serengeti; Murchison Falls; Masai Mara.

THICK-TAILED BUSHBABY *Otolemur crassicaudatus* TL 80 cm

Three species are currently recognized but all are very similar. Although usually observed in trees, when seen *on the ground it is superficially cat-like in appearance* but the rump is higher than the shoulders and the long, bushy tail is held high off the ground. The hair is woolly, fine and grey-brown in colour, and the underparts are lighter. The *large, rounded ears and large eyes* (that shine red in torchlight) are characteristic. Because of its nocturnal habits this primate is seldom seen but where it occurs its *loud, screaming call* is frequently heard. It occurs only in woodland, including forest and wooded river-banks. During the day it sleeps amongst dense vegetation, or in self-made nests in trees. It may lie up during the day in groups of up to six but at night it usually forages alone, although within the group's home range. The diet includes fruit, tree gums, insects, birds and lizards. A litter usually consists of two young.

Reserves: Hluhluwe-iMfolozi; uMkhuzi; Kruger; Mana Pools; Kafue; South Luangwa; Upemba; Ruaha; Mt Kilimanjaro; Serengeti; Masai Mara; Nairobi.

SOUTHERN LESSER GALAGO *Galago moholi* TL 40 cm

Lajuma Wilderness

There are at least eight species of small bushbabies in this area and all are similar in general appearance. This bushbaby (galago) could also be confused with the previous species but is *much smaller* and very rarely comes to the ground. The bushy tail is longer than the head and body length. Overall hair colour is grey to grey-brown with paler underparts, and the *large, forward-facing eyes are ringed with black*. This is a species of savanna woodland, and favours areas with acacia trees and riverine associations. It is entirely nocturnal and rests in self-constructed nests, tree holes and tangled vegetation, in groups of up to eight individuals. Each group occupies a home range of about 3 ha and defends a territory. They are *extremely agile* and adept jumpers. Tree sap and gum form the major part of their diet but they also eat insects. The young, either single or twins, weigh only 9 g at birth but the eyes are open and they are well haired.

Reserves: Kruger; Pilanesberg; Etosha; Moremi; Chobe; Hwange; Mana Pools; Kafue; South Luangwa; Upemba; Serengeti; Tsavo; Masai Mara; Nairobi; Amboseli. (Map includes this species and similar Senegal Galago.)

GROUND PANGOLIN *Manis (Smutsia) temminckii* TL 70 cm–1.0 m

This is one of two species of Ground Pangolins occurring in Africa. Also known as the Scaly Anteater, it is characterized by *large, brown scales* that cover the upperparts, sides and tail, and so cannot be mistaken for any other species. The *head is tiny and pointed* and the massively developed hindlegs and tail enable it to keep the forelimbs off the ground when walking. It occurs in many habitat types but is absent from forest and true desert. The distribution of its food – certain species of ants and termites – is probably the major determining factor of its distribution. *When threatened, the Pangolin curls itself into a tight ball*, the heavy scales protecting the vulnerable underparts. It rests up in dense foliage, in self-excavated burrows as well as in those excavated by other species. Most activity takes place at night but they do move during the day on occasion. A single young is born during the winter.

Reserves: Kruger; Etosha; Kgalagadi; Chobe; Hwange; Mana Pools; Serengeti; Marsabit; Masai Mara.

HARES AND RABBITS Order Lagomorpha

These mammals are characterized by having very well-developed hindlimbs and long ears, both of which are particularly noticeable in the hares. At least eight species occur in the area.

RIVERINE RABBIT *Bunolagus monticularis* TL 52 cm

This is one of Africa's rarest mammal species, occurring only in a limited area of the Karoo plains. It is similar to the red rock rabbits but the ears are longer and the hindlimbs more developed. The upperparts are grizzled-grey in colour with a deep red-brown patch of hair at the base of the ears. *A dark brown stripe runs along either side of the lower jaw to the ear bases.* The short, fluffy tail is uniform grey-brown. This rare rabbit is *restricted to riverine scrub.*

Karoo Images

Reserves: None.

SMITH'S RED ROCK RABBIT *Pronolagus rupestris* TL 54 cm

Four species of red rock rabbits occur in the region and all are similar in appearance. This species has fine fur, which is reddish-brown grizzled with grey, and the *rump and hindlegs are reddish.* The *tail is usually red-brown with a black tip.* As the common name implies rock rabbits are restricted to rocky habitats, and they are predominantly nocturnal although they will sun bask. They consume a wide variety of plants but predominantly grass. One to two helpless young are born in a nest lined with the belly fur of the mother.

Reserves: Karoo; Mountain Zebra; Camdeboo; Mokala; Tankwa; Augrabies; Willem Pretorius; Ngorongoro; Serengeti.

SCRUB HARE *Lepus saxatilis* TL 60 cm

SAVANNA HARE *Lepus microtis* TL 65 cm

These two species are indistinguishable in the field but Scrub Hare is restricted to western South Africa. Difficult to distinguish from the Cape Hare in the field but in most areas the Scrub Hare is larger, although it does vary in size from region to region, the largest animals occurring in the extreme south-west. The *ears are very long* and the hindlegs are extremely well developed. Both species have a short, fluffy tail that is black above and white below. The soft fur on the upperparts varies from brown-grey to grey with black flecking, and the underparts are white. A *white spot is usually present on the forehead.* This species is associated with *open woodland and scrub cover* and is often found in cultivated lands. Although mainly a solitary animal it may occur in high densities at a rich food source, feeding in loose association. Nearly all activity takes place at night, when it emerges to feed mainly on grasses, although other plants are taken. A litter usually comprises one to three well-developed young and these may be dropped at any time of the year.

Reserves: Bontebok; Mountain Zebra; Willem Pretorius; Hluhluwe-iMfolozi; Kruger; Pilanesberg; Kgalagadi; Etosha; Moremi; Chobe; Hwange; Mana Pools; Kafue; South Luangwa; Tsavo; Ngorongoro; Serengeti; Virunga; Masai Mara; Nairobi; Meru; Samburu. (Map shows range of *L. saxatilis* in south; *L. microtis* in east and west.)

CAPE HARE *Lepus capensis* TL 52 cm

Weighing up to only 2 kg, this hare is typical of the *Lepus* group in appearance. It is variable in colour, ranging from greyish-white to medium brown, the latter with a *reddish tinge along the sides* of the body. The chest is paler than the upperparts, and the belly is white. This species is associated with open habitats, such as grassland, and it avoids dense scrub. Feeding activity usually begins after sundown but it may feed longer on cool days. Grass forms the bulk of its diet but it will also feed from shrubs and bushes. Cape Hares are predominantly nocturnal, although occasionally crepuscular. During the day they lie up in a form (area of flattened grass conforming to the hare's shape) located in a grass clump or under a bush. Although a solitary species, several males may come together in association with an oestrus female. One to three young may be born at any time of year.

Reserves: Karoo; Willem Pretorius; Kruger; Kgalagadi; Namib-Naukluft; Etosha; Upemba; Serengeti; Tsavo; Masai Mara.

ROCK HYRAX (DASSIE) *Procavia capensis* TL 54 cm

 Five species of hyrax occur in this area, two restricted to rocky habitats and three are predominantly tree-dwellers. Many subspecies and races are recognized. The Rock Hyrax is small (2.5–4.6 kg) and stoutly built with *no visible tail*, and short, rounded ears. Pelage colour is very variable, even within a single colony, and ranges from yellow-fawn to dark brown. A *patch of erectile hair*, black in this species, is located *in the centre of the back* and is very important in distinguishing different species. This is a species of rocky habitats, including mountains, isolated outcrops and sea cliffs. In areas where they are very abundant they spread on to adjacent flatland where they shelter in erosion gullies and amongst dense vegetation. Predominantly diurnal, they do, however, feed on warm, moonlit nights. They live together in small groups, with many small colonies living in close proximity. Group density is dependent on food availability and adequate shelter. Each group has a dominant male and female and there is clearly demarcated social ranking. Hyrax eat a wide variety of plants. The well-developed young are able to move around soon after birth. A litter may comprise as many as four young, although two to three is usual.

Reserves: Table Mountain; Bontebok; Karoo; Mountain Zebra; uKhahlamba; Willem Pretorius; Kruger; Pilanesberg; Mt Kenya; Mt Kilimanjaro.

Note: *Other species occur in East and central Africa. Although this hyrax is sometimes called a Rock Rabbit, it is not related to the hares and rabbits.*

RODENTS Order Rodentia

This is a vast and diverse group of mammals that is well represented in Africa. Rodents are the only mammals with a large, prominent pair of chisel-like incisor teeth at the front of the upper and lower jaws.

PORCUPINE *Hystrix africaeaustralis* TL 86 cm

Two species of porcupine occur in the area that are very similar in appearance. The Porcupine is the largest African rodent (up to 24 kg) and cannot be mistaken for any other species. It has *an upper body covering of long, black and white banded quills and a crest of very long, coarse hair* extending from the top of the head to the shoulders, which it raises when alarmed. It occurs in most habitats but is usually most abundant in broken country. A nocturnal animal, it lies up during the day in self-excavated burrows, in caves or amongst rocks. Although it is mainly a solitary forager, pairs and family groups are quite common. Porcupines make use of regular pathways that are characterized by cast quills and shallow excavations. Their diet comprises many plant species, including bulbs, tubers and tree bark. Litters consist of one or two well-developed young that are born mainly during the summer.

Reserves: Virtually all.

SPRINGHARE *Pedetes capensis/surdaster* TL 80 cm

Despite its name this is a true rodent and not a hare. It is *kangaroo-like* in appearance, with long, *powerfully built hindlegs* and tiny forelegs used only for digging. They move by hopping on the hindlegs which have three of the four toes well developed and with large claws. The *tail is long and bushy* with a black tip, and the ears are long and pointed. The ears can be folded back to prevent sand and dust entering the passage, and the nostrils can be closed for the same reason. The soft fur of the upperparts is reddish-fawn to yellow and the underparts are paler. Springhares occur in areas of open grassland and sparse scrub-cover where there are compact, sandy soils. They are exclusively nocturnal and live in loose colonies, excavating their own burrows. Their main food consists of grass and roots and they do not move far from their burrows when feeding. In some areas they are a problem in croplands and pastures, and in many areas are considered excellent eating: in Botswana more than two million are harvested each year. A single, well-developed young (300 g) may be born at any time of the year and only emerges from the burrow after it is six weeks old.

Reserves: Mountain Zebra; Kruger; Pilanesberg; Kgalagadi; Etosha; Chobe; Hwange; Kafue; Serengeti; Masai Mara; Amboseli.

Note: *The Springhare in East Africa is now classified as a separate species,* Pedetes surdaster, *and differs in some behavioural aspects from its southern African cousin.*

CAPE DUNE MOLERAT *Bathyergus suillus* TL 32 cm

This is the *largest molerat* in our area, with a mass of up to 750 g. It has very soft, short fur, a short, dorso-ventrally flattened tail and a large, rounded head with a *flattened pig-like snout* and prominent incisors. The *eyes and ear openings are tiny*. Fur colour is variable but is usually cinnamon or pale fawn above with lighter underparts. This species is restricted to loose, sandy soils. It digs extensive burrow-systems which are indicated on the surface by large mounds of earth. Several animals share a set of burrows. It feeds on a wide range of roots, bulbs and tubers.

Reserves: Table Mountain; De Hoop; West Coast; Garden Route.

CAPE MOLERAT *Georychus capensis* TL 20 cm

Although similar to the other molerats, this species can be identified by the distinct *black and white markings on the head*. It has a mass of about 180 g, but some individuals of 360 g have also been recorded. The Cape Molerat occurs in loose soils and its habits are probably similar to those of other molerats.

Reserves: West Coast; Agulhas; Garden Route.

SOUTHERN AFRICAN GROUND SQUIRREL
Xerus inauris TL 45 cm

Of the four species of ground squirrel occurring in the area, this is by far the most abundant and widespread in the south. It is a terrestrial, burrowing rodent with an average mass of 650 g. The bushy tail is about half of the total length. *Hair on the upperparts is cinnamon brown, and a single white stripe runs along each side of the body from shoulder to thigh.* The underparts are lighter in colour. Ground Squirrels live in colonies of five to 30 individuals, which excavate their own extensive burrows. They feed on a variety of plants but will also eat termites on occasion. The young (one to three per litter) have a mass of 20 g at birth and only leave the burrow when about six weeks old.

Reserves: Willem Pretorius; Mokala; Augrabies; Kgalagadi; Namib-Naukluft; Etosha.

Note: *Three species of ground squirrels with pale lateral stripes occur in the area covered by this book and all are very similar in appearance and habits. Apart from the species described above, there is the Damara Ground Squirrel (Xerus princeps) which is restricted to western Namibia and south-western Angola; and the Striped Ground Squirrel (X. erythropus), which is widely distributed in western Kenya and Uganda. A similar species, but one which lacks the lateral stripe, is the Unstriped Ground Squirrel (X. rutilus), which is found throughout Kenya, Uganda and NE Tanzania.*

TREE SQUIRREL *Paraxerus cepapi* TL 35 cm

The tree squirrels are a very rich and diverse group in this part of Africa, comprising approximately 18 species. This species is one of the most common and widespread and is often associated with human habitation. It is *small* (180 g) and very variable in colour, from pale grey-brown to yellow-brown with pale fawn to white underparts. Although it inhabits many types of woodland it does not occur in true forest. A number of animals live in loose association and the adult male (or males) aggressively defends a territory against other squirrels. It is *very vocal, emitting a high-pitched screech which is accompanied by tail flicking.* It eats a wide range of plants, as well as insects.

Reserves: Kruger; Etosha; Moremi; Chobe; Hwange; Mana Pools; Kafue; South Luangwa; Upemba; Gombe Stream.

SPECTACLED DORMOUSE *Graphiurus ocularis* TL 25 cm

Of the at least 10 species of dormice in the area, the Spectacled Dormouse is one of the largest (80 g) and most attractive. It has a bushy, *squirrel-like tail,* and silvery-grey hair with lighter underparts. The *black and white facial markings* are distinctive. It is usually found in rocky habitats though may be found in association with trees and buildings. It is a nocturnal animal, very active, and possibly hibernates during cold periods. It eats both plant and animal food.

Reserves: Karoo; Camdeboo; Tankwa; Namaqua.

HAIRY-FOOTED GERBIL *Gerbillurus paeba* TL 20 cm

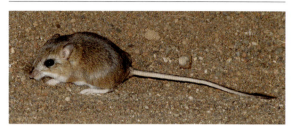

This is the most widely distributed species of the hairy-footed gerbils occurring in the south. It is small (25 g) and the tail makes up more than half of the total length. As the common name suggests, the soles of the feet are hairy. The upperparts may be greyish-red to reddish-brown but the underparts are always white. Hairy-footed gerbils occur in many habitats but sandy soils are a prerequisite. They feed mainly on seeds but also take insects. There are two to five young per litter.

Reserves: Bontebok; Karoo; Addo Elephant; Kgalagadi; Augrabies; Namib-Naukluft; Etosha; Chobe.

CAPE GERBIL *Gerbilliscus afra* TL 30 cm

The gerbils belonging to this group are large, this particular species having a mass of about 100 g. It has fairly long, woolly hair which is usually pale fawn with *brown mottling* on the upperparts; the underparts are paler to white. The *hindlegs and feet are well developed* and the ears are large and rounded. It is restricted to sandy areas where it excavates its own burrows and lives in colonies. Grass-seed makes up the bulk of its diet.

Reserves: Table Mountain; Bontebok; West Coast; Agulhas.

BUSHVELD GERBIL *Gerbilliscus leucogaster* TL 28 cm

The colour of the upperparts varies from *yellowish-brown to reddish-brown* but it is otherwise similar to the previous species. The tail has a distinct dark line along the upperside. Sandy soils are a requirement but otherwise this species has a wide habitat tolerance. It lives in loosely knit colonies. About five young are born per litter.

Reserves: Kruger; Pilanesberg; Kgalagadi; Etosha; Moremi; Chobe; Hwange; Mana Pools.

CAPE SHORT-TAILED GERBIL *Desmodillus auricularis* TL 20 cm

The Short-tailed Gerbil is the only gerbil with a tail that is shorter (9 cm) than its body length. It has a *dumpy, somewhat hamster-like appearance*. The upperparts are variable in colour, ranging from grey-brown to reddish-brown and the underparts are white. There is *a prominent white patch at the base of each ear*. This species shows a marked preference for hard ground in areas with short vegetation. Unlike other gerbils it does not live in dense colonies. Litters of one to seven young may be dropped at any time of the year.

Reserves: Karoo; Mountain Zebra; Kgalagadi; Namib-Naukluft; Etosha.

HOUSE RAT *Rattus rattus* TL 37 cm

An introduced species, this large rat is often *found in association with human settlements*. Where this species lives in buildings it establishes fixed pathways, which are distinguished by greasy smears located at corners and narrow gaps. The House Rat is typically rat-like in appearance and the long (20 cm), heavy tail is prominently scaled. The feet are large, as are the thin, rounded ears. Colour varies from grey-brown to black and the underparts are grey to white. It is a very successful rodent and digs well, swims and is adept at climbing. It eats virtually anything and is considered one of the most important pest species in the world.

Reserves: None known.

VLEI RAT *Otomys irroratus* TL 24 cm

There are about 14 species in the genus *Otomys* and all are very similar in appearance. They are *robust, stocky rats with a short tail* (9 cm), a blunt muzzle and rounded ears. The overall body colour is variable but is usually very dark slate-grey with a brownish tinge and the underparts are somewhat paler. This species is closely associated with moist, marshy areas but on occasion may be found on densely grassed hill slopes. They are mainly active during the day, and their presence in an area is indicated by the numerous runways, small piles of cut grass and reed stems, and cylindrical droppings.

Reserves: Table Mountain; Bontebok; Karoo; Mountain Zebra; Addo Elephant; uKhahlamba; Willem Pretorius; Hluhluwe-iMfolozi.

GAMBIAN GIANT RAT *Cricetomys gambianus* TL 80 cm

This is a massive (1–3 kg) 'rat-like' rodent, with a *distinctive long, whip-like tail that is white along half of its length towards the tip*. The upperparts are grey to grey-brown and the underparts are paler. There is a dark ring around the eyes and the ears are long, rounded and thin. Although a species of forest and woodland, it is sometimes found in association with urban areas. It is mainly nocturnal but daylight activity is not unusual. Although it digs its own burrows, it will lie up in many different situations. Despite its size it is placid and harmless. The Gambian Giant Rat feeds mainly on fruits, seeds and roots.

Reserves: Ndumo; Mana Pools; Kasanka; Shimba Hills.

DASSIE RAT *Petromus typicus* TL 30 cm

This *squirrel-like* rodent has a hairy but not bushy tail, and short, rounded ears. The upperparts are grizzled grey-brown with the hindquarters being more uniformly brown and the underparts lighter in colour. It is restricted to rocky areas in the arid west, where it can be seen basking in the early morning sunshine. Normally it lives in pairs or family groups which spend the nights in deep rock crevices. Although it favours green plant material it also feeds on seeds, flowers and twigs, and food is usually carried to shelter.

Reserves: Namib-Naukluft; Augrabies; Namaqua.

GREY CLIMBING MOUSE *Dendromus melanotis* TL 15 cm

Grey Climbing Mouse

This small (8 g) mouse is one of six species of climbing mice in the area. All are characterized by a *very long tail (8–10 cm) and a dark, diffused, dorsal stripe*. The ash-grey fur may be browner on the shoulders, neck and head. Underparts are white. All live in habitats with long grass, reedbeds or dense vegetation, where they can put to good use their climbing adaptations, semi-prehensile tails and gripping toes. They feed mainly on seeds and insects. In common with other climbing mice, this species builds a small, ball-shaped nest of fine grass, which may be located above, or below, the ground. It has been reported that they will make use of weaver nests as well as burrows under rocks. Litters of two to eight helpless young are born in summer.

Reserves: Bontebok; Addo Elephant; Mokala; Kruger.

CAPE SPINY MOUSE *Acomys subspinosus* TL 17 cm

There are four species of spiny mice in the area, all of which have *spiny dorsal hairs*. Their form is typically mouse-like and the upperparts are normally dark grey-brown and the underparts white. This species is restricted to rocky habitats and is active mainly at night. It eats seeds, green plant material and insects. Two to five young are born per litter in summer.

Reserves: Table Mountain; Garden Route; Baviaanskloof; Addo Elephant.

POUCHED MOUSE *Saccostomus campestris* TL 15 cm

With its round, fat body this species *closely resembles the domestic hamster in general appearance.* The soft, silky fur is grey to greyish-brown above and the underparts and lower face are white. The short tail is only about one-third of the total length. One of the main characteristics of this mouse is its ability to carry large quantities of food in its cheek-pouches. Although it digs its own burrows, it will also use a wide variety of other shelters. Seeds and small fruits form the bulk of its diet but it will also eat insects. As many as 10 well-developed young may be born in the wet summer months.

Reserves: Mountain Zebra; Karoo; Camdeboo; Garden Route; Kruger; Kgalagadi; Etosha; Chobe; Hwange; Mana Pools.

FAT MOUSE *Steatomys pratensis* TL 13 cm

All of the fat mice species are similar in appearance and difficult to distinguish in the field. Like its relatives, it has a *short tail* (5 cm) which in this species is darker above than below. The upperparts of the body are rusty-brown with a distinct sheen and the underparts are white. As it

digs its own burrows, it shows a marked preference for sandy soils. Fat Mice derive their name from their ability to store large quantities of body fat to carry them over periods of food shortage. Seeds make up most of their food intake. Litters of one to nine young have been recorded and are dropped during the summer months.

Reserves: uMkhuzi; Kruger; Etosha; Moremi; Chobe; Hwange; Mana Pools.

NAMAQUA ROCK MOUSE *Aethomys namaquensis* TL 26 cm

Another typical mouse-like species with a tail that is more than half of the total length. Coloration is very variable but is usually reddish-brown to yellowish-fawn, with greyish-white to white underparts. There are no distinctive markings. As the common name suggests it is restricted to *rocky habitats*, living in small colonies in rock crevices. The entrances to the nests are often piled with dry grass and other plant debris. The young are born during summer.

Reserves: Virtually all in the south.

FOUR-STRIPED GRASS MOUSE *Rhabdomys pumilio* TL 20 cm

This *diurnal*, clearly marked mouse is easy to observe in some areas. The overall body colour varies from grey-white to dark russet-brown but it is distinguished from other species by the *four longitudinal stripes running down the back*. The underparts may be dirty off-white to pale grey-brown. The *backs of the ears are reddish-brown to yellow-brown*. It has a very wide habitat tolerance as long as grass is present. Burrows have many runways radiating from them.

Reserves: Table Mountain; Bontebok; Karoo; Mountain Zebra; Addo Elephant; uKhahlamba; Willem Pretorius; Pilanesberg; Kgalagadi; Namib-Naukiuft; Etosha.

PYGMY MOUSE *Mus minutoides* TL 10 cm

There are about 10 species of pygmy mice in the area and all are similar with a typical mouse-like appearance. This mouse is *tiny* (6 g) and the tail is shorter than the head and body length. The underparts are always white but the upperparts range from grey-brown to red-brown in colour. The upper surfaces of the hands and feet are off-white. It occupies a wide range of habitats but it is absent from very dry areas. The Pygmy Mouse is nocturnal and feeds mainly on seeds. Colonies are not formed as it lives singly or in family groups. Litters of one to seven young are dropped in the summer after a gestation period of only 19 days.

Reserves: Table Mountain; Bontebok; Mountain Zebra; Addo Elephant; uKhahlamba; Willem Pretorius; Hluhluwe-iMfolozi; uMkhuzi; Kruger; Mana Pools.

VERREAUX'S MOUSE *Mastomys verreauxii* TL 25 cm

This 'typical' mouse is a member of a species complex that is difficult for even the specialist to distinguish. In this species the tail is slightly longer than the head and body length. The upperparts are uniformly grey to grey-brown in colour, the underparts are paler, and the upper surfaces of the hands and feet are white. There is a *dark ring around the eyes*. It is usually associated with wet habitats and with fairly dense vegetation cover but is commonly found in and around buildings. Seeds, fruit and insects all form part of the diet.

Reserves: Table Mountain; Bontebok; Agulhas; West Coast.

ELEPHANT SHREWS (SENGIS)
Family Macroscelididae TL 21–50 cm

At least 17 species of elephant shrew, or sengi, occur in the area, several restricted to rocky habitats, some to forest and woodland, and others to open scrub plains. All species are similar in appearance and derive their common name from the elongated, trunk-like snout, which is constantly twitching. The ears are large, the eyes prominent and, in most species, ringed with short white hair. The hair is soft and the upperparts are usually grey or grey-brown to russet in colour, with the exception of the Chequered Elephant Shrew, which is white and fawn, and the Golden-rumped Elephant Shrew. The hindlegs and feet are much more developed than the front limbs. Elephant shrews are predominantly diurnal, terrestrial and solitary. All species are insectivores, often showing a preference for ants and termites. The newborn young are well developed at birth.

WESTERN ROCK SENGI *Elephantulus rupestris* TL 28 cm

The upperparts are straw-yellow-fawn to brown but *strongly pencilled with black. Patches of reddish-yellow hair* are located at the base of the ears and extend on to the nape. The underparts are greyish-white, and *narrow, white rings rim the eyes*. As the common name implies this is a species of *rocky habitats*. It is predominantly diurnal but is also active on warm, moonlit nights. It hunts from the shade, making short dashes out to catch insects, and carrying large prey back to its shelter. This elephant shrew is often found in association with Dassie (Rock Hyrax) dung middens where it feeds on insects such as flies. In common with other elephant shrews it is very alert and flees at the slightest disturbance.

Reserves: Mountain Zebra; Etosha; Namib-Naukluft; Augrabies.

ROUND-EARED SENGI *Macroscelides proboscideus* TL 23 cm

In this species coloration is very variable, from pale creamy-grey to brownish-grey but there is *no white eye-ring*. The ears are shorter than in other species and are rounded at the tips. This is a species of open *gravel plains*, occurring where there is some bush cover and where soils are soft enough to allow for short, shallow burrows. They are most active during dawn, dusk and at night, but can also be observed during the day sunning themselves close to cover. Hunting pathways radiate in all directions from their shelters and these are characterized by evenly spaced bare patches created by their bounding gait.

Reserves: Karoo; Namaqua; Tankwa; Mountain Zebra; Camdeboo; Kgalagadi; Namib-Naukluft.

GOLDEN-RUMPED SENGI *Rhynchocyon chrysopygus* TL 50 cm

K. Rudloff

This large (550 g) elephant shrew is rich tawny on the upperparts with a distinctive *golden-yellow rump*, long legs and a trunk-like snout. The *feet, legs, ears and much of the tail are black*, the latter being white on its outer third but with a black tip. A *short crest* extends from between the ears to the shoulders. It inhabits moist, dense coastal scrub, forest and woodland. Males and females form monogamous pairs and live in adjoining home ranges. The pairs defend the home range, the female chasing females and the male driving away only males. Their diet includes grasshoppers, beetles, spiders, millipedes and earthworms. A single young, weighing about 80 g, may be born at any time of the year.

Reserves: Sokoke.

SHREWS Family Soricidae TL 8–25 cm

Probably as many as 100 species of shrew have been recorded within the area covered by this book, the majority belonging to the genus *Crocidura*, but it is likely that new species will be recorded in the future. They are divided into several groups but the non-specialist will experience great difficulty in identifying them to species level. All species are small and mouse-like, with long, wedge-shaped heads, tiny eyes and small ears. In most species the tail is shorter than the head and body length and the legs are short. Most are dark in colour and the fur is short and soft. For their size (3.5–110 g) they are very aggressive and at least some species vigorously defend a territory. All eat insects and other invertebrates, as well as the occasional small lizard or mouse. From two to six naked and helpless young are born, mainly in the warm, wet season.

FOREST SHREW *Myosorex varius* TL 12 cm

All members of this genus have *short-haired tails, lacking the long bristles* of the musk and dwarf shrews. The upperparts are dark grey to almost black in colour, and the underparts are pale grey and often have a brownish tinge. The upper surfaces of the feet are grey. This shrew is restricted to moist, densely vegetated habitats where it is active for periods throughout the day and night. It is an active but shallow burrower and constructs soft grass nests with one or more entrances. The Forest Shrew may occur in very high densities in suitable habitats and in some areas uses the same pathways as the Four-striped Grass Mouse.

Reserves: Table Mountain; Bontebok; Karoo; Mountain Zebra; Addo Elephant; uKhahlamba; Willem Pretorius; Hluhluwe-Umfolozi; uMkhuzi.

REDDISH-GREY MUSK SHREW *Crocidura cyanea* TL 13 cm

This small (8.5 g) shrew is very variable in colour but is commonly grey with a reddish-brown tint, evident to a greater or lesser extent. The fur is grizzled and the underparts are paler than the upperparts. These shrews can be separated from the *Myosorex* group by the presence of *long bristles along much of the length of the tail*. They inhabit high- and low-rainfall areas.

Reserves: Table Mountain; Bontebok; Karoo; Mountain Zebra; Addo Elephant; uKhahlamba; Willem Pretorius; Hluhluwe-iMfolozi; uMkhuzi; Kruger; Pilanesberg; Chobe; Hwange; Mana Pools.

Note: *Also extensively distributed in Central and East Africa.*

LESSER DWARF SHREW *Suncus varilla* TL 9 cm

This is a very small shrew (6.5 g) with greyish-fawn upperparts and *sharply demarcated*, pale silvery-fawn *underparts*. The upper surfaces of the hands and feet are white, and there are *long bristles along the length of the tail*. It occurs in a wide range of habitats and is often associated with sandy soils and termite mounds.

Reserves: Mountain Zebra; uKhahlamba; Willem Pretorius.

GOLDEN MOLES Family Chrysochloridae TL 7–23 cm

The family of golden moles, comprising 21 species in all (18 in southern Africa), occurs on the African continent only. Very little is known about these small insectivores, however, because they *live underground*. All species are very similar in appearance: most have soft, *silky hair* and are noted for the *absence of visible eyes, ears or tail*. The snouts are tipped with a leathery pad which, in conjunction with the well-developed front claws, is used for digging. Golden moles excavate long, meandering tunnels that show as rounded ridges on the surface, and a few species push up surface heaps. All species show a strong preference for sandy or loamy soils, and usually avoid clay-type soils. They feed on a wide range of insects, earthworms and small subterranean reptiles. One or two helpless and naked young are born mainly in the rainy season.

HOTTENTOT GOLDEN MOLE *Amblysomus hottentotus* TL 13 cm

The upperparts are rich *dark reddish-brown* with an obvious *bronze sheen* and are usually tinged with purplish-green. Although similar in colour the underparts lack the bronze sheen. The cheeks are usually off-white to yellow-brown. The hindfeet are webbed as an aid to shovelling soft soil that is excavated by the snout and by the well-developed claws on the front feet. This species shows a marked preference for higher rainfall areas with grassland and is absent from arid regions. It is most obviously active during warm, wet periods and it is at this time that the young, weighing 4.5 g, are born. This species is predominantly insectivorous but will also eat bulbs on occasion. Unlike the rodent molerats, these mammals do no damage to crops.

Reserves: Addo Elephant; uKhahlamba; Hluhluwe-iMfolozi.

HEDGEHOGS Family Erinaceidae

SOUTHERN AFRICAN HEDGEHOG *Atelerix frontalis* TL 20 cm

One of two species of hedgehog occurring in the area covered by this book, this small (400 g) insectivore is easy to identify. The upperparts are covered with *short but sharp, banded spines* extending from the forehead over the back to the rump. Dark hair covers the face, legs and the short tail but a *prominent band of white hair* extends across the forehead and beyond the ears. It has a wide habitat tolerance but is absent from desert and regions with high rainfall. During the day it lies up in burrows dug by other species or amongst dry vegetation. Little is known about hibernation in this species but it would seem that it rests up between May and July, with most activity taking place during the wet summer months when food is most abundant. It feeds on a wide range of insects, earthworms, lizards, mice and wild fruits, and it is a solitary animal, except when a female is accompanied by young. The young weigh only 10 g at birth and have a complete covering of spines only at about six weeks of age. When threatened hedgehogs curl into a tight ball, the outward-pointing spines protecting the vulnerable underparts and head. Many of these appealing animals are killed on roads, illegally kept as pets and hunted for food in some regions. Although their spines repel most predators they are frequently caught by the Giant Eagle-owl, with its long talons and hard, scaly feet. The other hedgehog in the area, *A. albiventris*, has a white head and underparts and occurs in East African savanna and semi-arid country. It is most frequently encountered on sandy terrain.

Reserves: Mountain Zebra; Willem Pretorius; Etosha; Hwange.

BATS Order Chiroptera

The bats are the only true flying mammals and are divided into two major groups: the fruit-eating bats or Megachiroptera and the insect-eating bats belonging to the Microchiroptera. The fruit-eating bats are generally much larger in size than those in the insect-eating group. Approximately 20 fruit-eating bat species and more than 100 insect-eating bats occur in southern, Central and East Africa but there is the distinct possibility that a number of new species will be described in the future.

EGYPTIAN FRUIT-BAT *Rousettus aegyptiacus* WS 60 cm

The fruit-bats have *pointed, dog-like heads* and a *very short tail*. The Egyptian Fruit-bat has dark brown upperparts and grey-brown underparts and has no distinct or obvious markings. As with all fruit-bats the *eyes are large* but this species is alone in its *ability to use echo-location* – an obvious advantage in its cave-roosts where it utilizes the darkest areas. Roosts may contain from a few hundred to several thousand individuals and noise levels are very high. This species favours forested areas or savanna and riverine woodland where food is plentiful. It

feeds on a wide range of ripe wild and cultivated fruits, the latter bringing it into conflict with farmers. The fruit-eating bats play a critical role in the dispersal of tree seeds and pollination of others. It has been estimated that a single fruit-bat can spread many thousands of seeds in a single night's feeding. Without bats the Baobab would probably die out as they are its principal pollinators. As a result a whole chain of extinctions could result. For the first six weeks of life the single young is carried by the mother, then it is left at the roost until it can forage on its own.

Reserves: Garden Route; Addo Elephant; iSimangaliso; uMkhuzi; Kruger; Mana Pools.

Note: *Also ranges widely to the north but occurrence in specific reserves unknown.*

WAHLBERG'S EPAULETTED FRUIT-BAT
Epomophorus wahlbergi WS 50 cm

The epauletted fruit-bats, of which there are several species, are distinguished by the *white patches at the base of the ears* and by the glandular pouches on the shoulders of the males, which are covered by long, white hair. Hair colour is variable but the upperparts are usually buffy-brown to darker brown, and the underparts are paler. Unlike the previous species this bat *roosts in trees*, often in large numbers and in association with other epauletted fruit-bat species. It is largely restricted to forest and riverine woodland wherever there are suitable fruit-bearing trees. Many species of fruit-bat are subject to local or long-distance movements in search of fruit. Most young are born during the summer.

Reserves: iSimangaliso; Hluhluwe-iMfolozi; uMkhuzi; Ndumo; Kruger.

Note: *Many to the north but specifics unknown.*

MAURITIAN TOMB BAT *Taphozous mauritianus* WS 34 cm

This insectivorous bat is easy to identify with its *large eyes* (unusual in insect-eating bats), *pure white underparts* and its *sheathed tail*. More than half of the tail is enclosed by the tail membrane, the remainder being free. The tail tip does not reach the outer edge of the membrane, however, thus distinguishing it from the free-tailed bats. A species of woodland savanna, it usually occurs in pairs and is often seen hanging to the outer walls of buildings and tree trunks. It is a fast flyer and hunts mainly at night but has been observed foraging during the day. A single young is born in summer.

Reserves: iSimangaliso; Kruger; Hwange, Mana Pools.

SUNDEVALL'S LEAF-NOSED BAT *Hipposideros caffer* WS 20 cm

E. Seamark

A small, leaf-nosed bat with simple nose-leaves that bear some resemblance to those of the horseshoe bats, but not as elaborate. Coloration is variable but is usually dark grey-brown above and slightly paler below. The fur is long and woolly. This is a species that inhabits woodland savanna. It roosts in many different locations and may congregate in groups of five to several hundred individuals. A single young is born in summer.

Reserves: iSimangaliso; uMkhuzi; Kruger; Etosha; Mana Pools.

EGYPTIAN SLIT-FACED BAT *Nycteris thebaica* WS 24 cm

There are 10 species of slit-faced bat in the area, all similar in appearance. They have a *long, lobed slit* running down the centre of the face and the *ears are long* (3.4 cm in this species), erect and parallel-sided. The tip of the tail is shallowly forked. The upperparts are usually buffy-brown but may vary from greyish-white to reddish; the underparts are paler. A species with a wide habitat tolerance, it may be found roosting in many different places, including buildings. Roosts may consist of a few individuals to several hundred. Prey is captured and carried to fixed feeding sites which can be identified by the litter of inedible debris such as moth wings, grasshopper legs and beetle elytra.

Reserves: Karoo; Hluhluwe-iMfolozi; uMkhuzi; Kruger; Pilanesberg; Kgalagadi; Namib-Naukluft; Etosha; Moremi; Chobe; Hwange; Mana Pools.

GEOFFROY'S HORSESHOE BAT *Rhinolophus clivosus* WS 32 cm

There are at least 20 species of horseshoe bat known to occur in the area covered by this book and all are very similar in appearance and require detailed examination to identify to species level. The horseshoe bats derive their name from the *horseshoe-shaped main nose-leaf* that is situated above the upper lip. Two skin outgrowths, known as the *sella* and *lancet,* are also located on the face. The outer edge of the tail membrane is more-or-less squared off. Geoffroy's Horseshoe Bat is one of the largest species, and has light brown but somewhat blotchy upperparts and paler underparts. The wing and tail membranes are dark brown. Although it shows a preference for savanna woodland it has been recorded from many different habitats. This is a cave-rooster and may congregate in large colonies numbering many thousands. A single young is born in summer.

Reserves: Table Mountain; Karoo; Mountain Zebra; Hluhluwe-iMfolozi; Kruger; Namib-Naukluft; Etosha; Mana Pools.

CAPE SEROTINE BAT *Neoromicia capensis* WS 24 cm

This bat belongs to the family known as the Vespertilionidae, a very large and diverse group that also includes the following three species. All have simple, mouse-like muzzles and lack any prominent facial structures. The ears are well developed and the tail is enclosed by the membrane which is 'V'-shaped. The Cape Serotine is very variable both in size and coloration, which has led to the belief that in fact several unrecognized species may be involved. The wing membranes are usually blackish-brown. They roost in small numbers and are usually well hidden. A single young (sometimes twins) is born in summer.

Reserves: Virtually all.

TEMMINCK'S HAIRY BAT *Myotis tricolor* WS 28 cm

These small bats have pointed muzzles that distinguish them from other Vespertilionid bats. Six species occur throughout Africa. The *upperparts are pale coppery-red*, the underparts much paler, and the wing membranes are dark brown. The tail membrane also has a *covering of coppery-red hair*. This bat is absent from the dry west but otherwise shows a wide habitat tolerance. It roosts in small colonies in caves and mines and is often found in association with other bat species. It is a slow and generally low flier, catching insects in flight but other hairy bats are known to take insects off vegetation and the ground. Females have been recorded dropping a single young during October and November in the Western Cape province, South Africa.

Reserves: Table Mountain; Bontebok; Hluhluwe-iMfolozi; Kruger.

BANANA BAT *Neoromicia nanus* WS 19 cm

This species belongs to another group of bats, who are similar in appearance and difficult for non-specialists to distinguish. Pipistrelles, of which there are many similar species, occur worldwide and are characterized by their erratic, fluttering flight. The Banana Bat, one of the most common and widespread of the small bats in this genus in Africa, is *tiny* (4 g), with light to dark brown upperparts, slightly paler underparts, and brown wing and tail membranes. It frequently roosts in the tightly rolled leaves of banana and strelitzia plants, hence the name, and has developed pads on the wings and feet to cope with the steep, slippery surfaces. It is usually solitary, but also occurs in pairs or small groups, although it's limited by the nature of its principal roost. One or two young are born in summer.

Reserves: uMkhuze; Hluhluwe-iMfolozi; iSimangaliso; Kruger; Mana Pools; Kasanka; Masai-Mara.

AFRICAN YELLOW BAT *Scotophilus dinganii* WS 30 cm

The upperparts of this bat vary from light olive-brown to rich reddish-brown and the *underparts are usually bright to dull yellow* but can be much paler. The hair of the underparts extends broadly on to the wing membranes. This is a species of savanna woodland, roosting in small numbers in hollow trees and in the roofs of buildings. It is known to roost in woodpecker and barbet holes, and is commonly associated with human habitation. This fast, low-flying bat not infrequently enters houses to hawk insects around lights. It has been reported that beetles form an important part of its diet. Unlike most bats that give birth to a single young, the female Yellow House Bat usually has twins and commonly triplets.

Reserves: iSimangaliso; uMkhuzi; Kruger; Kgalagadi; Etosha; Chobe; Hwange.

EGYPTIAN FREE-TAILED BAT *Tadarida aegyptiaca* WS 30 cm

Twenty-eight species of free-tailed bat are known to occur in south, Central and East Africa and most are similar in appearance. As the name implies, they are characterized by a tail that is enclosed for one third to a half of its length in the tail membrane, with the remainder *extending beyond the edge of the membrane, mouse-like*. Also known as bulldog or mastiff bats, they have a short head with *heavy wrinkling on the upper lip*. This bat has dark grey-brown upperparts, although the top of the head and back is much darker and the membranes are lighter brown. It is present in virtually all habitats, roosting in many different places, and lives in small colonies. A single young is born during summer.

Reserves: Virtually all.

GLOSSARY

Aquatic: Living in or near water.
Arboreal: Adapted for life in trees.
Boss: Heavy horn mass at base of buffalo and wildebeest horns.
Browser: An animal that feeds mainly on woody or herbaceous plants.
Carnivore: An animal that preys on other animals for its food.
Cheek-teeth: Molar and premolar teeth lying behind canines or incisors.
Crepuscular: Active during the twilight hours of dawn and dusk.
Diurnal: Active during the daylight hours.
Endemic: Native to a particular region or restricted area.
Foraging: Searching for food.
Gestation period: The period between conception and birth in which offspring are carried in the uterus.
Grazer: An animal that eats mainly grass.
Herbivore: Any organism that feeds mainly on plants.
Home range: The area covered by an animal in the course of its day-to-day activities.
Incisors: Sharp-edged front teeth, usually in both upper and lower jaws.
Insectivore: A mammal that feeds mainly on insects.
Omnivore: An animal that eats both plant matter and meat.
Scrotum: The pouch that contains the testes of most male mammals.
Sounder: Collective name given to pigs.
Species: A group of interbreeding individuals of common ancestry, reproductively isolated from all other groups.
Territory: A restricted area inhabited by an animal, often for breeding purposes, and actively defended against other individuals of the same species.

SUGGESTED FURTHER READING

Dorst, J. & Dandelot, P. 1983. *A Field Guide to the Larger Mammals of Africa.* Collins, London.
Haltenorth, T. & Diller, H. 1984. *A Field Guide to the Mammals of Africa, including Madagascar.* Collins, London.
Kingdon, J. 1971-1982. *East African Mammals: an Atlas of Evolution in Africa.* (Vols 1–111). Academic Press, London.
Skinner, J. & Chimimba, C.T. 2005. *The Mammals of the Southern African Subregion.* Cambridge University Press, Cambridge.
Stuart, C. & T. 2006. *Field Guide to the Larger Mammals of Africa.* Struik Publishers, Cape Town.
Stuart, C. & T. 2007. *Field Guide to the Mammals of Southern Africa.* Struik Publishers, Cape Town.
Stuart, C. & M. 2012. *National Parks and Nature Reserves – A South African Field Guide.* Struik Travel & Heritage, Cape Town.
Stuart, C. & M. 2013. *A Field Guide to the Tracks and Signs of Southern, Central and East African Wildlife.* Struik Nature, Cape Town.

INDEX OF SCIENTIFIC NAMES

INDEX OF COMMON NAMES